Secrets to a
Successful
Marriage

Every Muslim Couple's Guide to a
Long and Contented Married Life

Afshan Khan (Umm Asim)

Edited by Leila Rajab-Ali

Ta-Ha Publishers Ltd

© 1436 AH/2015 CE Ta-Ha Publishers Ltd.
Reprinted, 2016

Published by:
Ta-Ha Publishers Ltd,
Unit 4, The Windsor Centre,
Windsor Grove, West Norwood,
London, SE27 9NT
United Kingdom

Website: www.tahapublishers.com
E-mail: support@tahapublishers.com

Written by: Afshan Khan (Umm Asim)
General Editor: Dr Abia Afsar-Siddiqui
Edited by: Leila Rajab-Ali and Affan Aziz
Cover/Book Design by: Shakir AbdulCadir, www.opensquares.uk

A catalogue record of this book is available from the British Library

ISBN: 978 184200 157 8

Printed and bound by: IMAK Ofset, Turkey

Dedication

I extend my gratefulness and appreciation to
my dear husband, my children and my daughter-in-law
for their support in helping me attain my vision.

Acknowledgments

In the name of Allah the Most Beneficent, the Most Merciful

⬿

My sincere gratitude to my mother, Shahnaz Naeem, who, alhamdulillah, gave me the solid foundation upon which I have been able to base my own family and my work, and to my family for their support and encouragement.

Thanks to my friend and colleague Umm Bilal, for her invaluable support in writing this book. I would also like to thank Leila Rajab-Ali for her dedication and commitment to seeing this project through.

All praise is to Allah, Lord of the Worlds, who has given me the means of helping my brothers and sisters in Islam.

"Men and women who are Muslims,

men and women who are believers,

men and women who are obedient,

men and women who are truthful,

men and women who are steadfast,

men and women who are humble,

men and women who give sadaqa,

men and women who fast,

men and women who guard their private parts,

men and women who remember Allah much:

Allah has prepared forgiveness for them

and an immense reward."

(Qur'an 33:35)

CONTENTS

Preface

✦

I am an Islamic counsellor and a relationship life coach with almost thirty years of experience and have dealt with many issues affecting our community. My work centres around marital issues, family disputes, teenage problems, domestic violence and mediation. Over the years, countless numbers of couples have come to me with their grievances and to seek solutions for their domestic discord. Many of these have a commonly recurring theme and, in many cases, the problems have a simple solution.

So much more thought needs to go into choosing a life partner and reviewing unrealistic expectations. Having secured a spouse, couples think that they can stop making an effort with each other, when in fact, this is when all the hard work begins. These issues play a big part in couples' disharmony, but can often be solved with greater communication and understanding from both parties.

This book was written on the basis of my experience with couples and the common issues that crop up. I hope that it will help couples to rethink their attitudes and encourage them to invest more into making their marriages successful and fulfilling.

Introduction

❧

One of the greatest values of Islam is that it is based on the strength of its community and the basic unit of that community is not the individual but the family unit. When that unit functions well and is a source of love and peace for all its members, then the community will be strong and can flourish. When marriages break down, however, the community becomes weaker.

The Shari'ah Council recently reported a 40% divorce rate (and rising) amongst Muslim couples. This is shockingly high but also avoidable. In my workshops and counselling sessions I meet many brothers and sisters who are frustrated and disappointed with their marriages. Lack of communication and misunderstanding over small issues, over time, snowball into causes of major anger and resentment. Marriage is no longer a source of tranquillity, but a source of stress. Some couples store their resentment and continue in unfulfilling marriages. Others divorce.

I have seen people who, in hindsight, regret acting in haste and getting divorced. If they could have their time again, they would give their marriage more of a chance. I also see many children of divorced couples who, as adults, are still suffering from the devastating effect of their parents' divorce decades ago. They are now carrying this baggage through into their own marriages and the cycle is repeating down the generations. But this is a cycle that must be broken, insha'Allah.

It is my sincere intention, in writing this book, to help our community overcome this fundamental issue. With thirty years' experience of counselling couples, I have gained an insight into the key factors that help a marriage be successful and the causes that can lead to disharmony. The advice and solutions that I have offered in my counselling sessions over the decades have worked to increase understanding between many, many couples and strengthen the marital bond, by the permission of Allah. I have gathered this experience and distilled it into this book, which I pray will be of use to all Muslim couples, whatever stage and state of their marriage, as prevention is always better than cure.

This book aims to address various aspects of marriage and there are four parts to it:

- *Finding 'the one'* focuses on pre-marriage. It might sound obvious, but looking for a spouse is a life decision and this is a crucial moment where you need to be honest, sincere, open and know what you want.
- *Keeping the love alive.* Marriage can be an evergreen garden when given tender loving care. Sometimes you need to pull out the weeds, sometimes water the flowers and devote time and care in order for the garden to flourish. It's the same with marriage. These chapters will show you how to tend your marriage to keep it successful, whether you are newly weds or a seasoned couple.

- *Reflecting on 'me' to improve 'us'.* Every relationship has its ups and downs and there will inevitably be periods of time when we feel less fulfilled within the marriage. This section will give both partners tips about how to get through these periods and emerge stronger than before. By strengthening yourself, you are able to strengthen and support each other and thus the marriage.
- *Putting things right* deals with more serious issues, how to recognise the signs of a serious problem within your marriage and, crucially, how to work through this without hurting each other.

As an Islamic counsellor, it is not my job to issue *fatwas* or to advise on matters of *fiqh*. However, through speaking with scholars and people of knowledge, and also my own study of Islam, I do include some basic Islamic advice. All Qur'anic quotes in this book are taken from Abdalhaqq and Aisha Bewley's The Noble Qur'an.

Through the grace of Allah, I pray that the advice given in this book will be a help to those single Muslims seeking a marriage partner, to those couples starting out on their journey and wanting to learn more about marriage, and for those that are looking for solutions for their less-than-ideal marriages.

❧❧❧

Chapter 1

Finding The One

Great Expectations

Fundamentally, the thing that will make or break a marriage is expectations. It is all very well having idealistic expectations, but when these are not met, then the result is discontentment and dissatisfaction, either because it is almost impossible to find a marriage partner in the first place or because your spouse can never live up to those sky-high expectations. Having grounded expectations that match with reality is a more sensible starting point for an endeavour as serious as marriage.

The first step to finding a marriage partner is to know what you want and what you need and applying those criteria when looking for a spouse. But it is not as easy as it sounds! You might be surprised to hear that the things that we think we want before marriage and the things that we actually want after marriage are often poles apart. For example, I've frequently found that potential husbands, whose fervent desire was to marry a pious woman, an *'alima* even, are actually really disappointed when she can't cook. Cooking and (the lack of) good housekeeping skills then become an issue in the marriage. Likewise, I frequently hear from women who ask for a man who is a good provider, but forget to ask for a man who demonstrates kindness and consideration in other ways.

Then there are those who don't really give it enough thought beforehand in the hope that everything will fall into place. Well as you can imagine, it is often the case that neither of these scenarios bode well for a good marriage.

So, we need to ask ourselves, what do we expect from marriage? This is a question that should be explored *before* we begin to view prospective partners in much the same way as you would plan a journey before setting off. It should be answered after self-reflection, with honesty and sincere intentions, and applies to both men and women alike.

It might sound obvious but life after marriage is very different from life before marriage and there needs to be a willingness to adapt and assume the new role with its own set of rights and responsibilities, as the case studies below demonstrate.

Case Study

Sister Sheba[1] came to me, complaining, "I've been married for six months and I miss my single life! I can't go shopping when I want, I have to come back from work and cook and clean. I don't do this routine thing very well." I asked her, "What did you expect from your marriage? Her response was, "I just didn't think it would be like this. I assumed things would just fall into place." "How?" I asked. "Before I got married I would leave work, go shopping, visit friends and when I got home mum would have dinner ready on the table for me." I asked her, "Did you not think marriage is about change, new roles and responsibilities, which have to be embraced?" She responded, "You're right, I should have thought about it but I was too busy planning the whole wedding and no one ever sat down and explained to me the responsibilities of being a wife."

Sheba and I spent the session identifying that the main issue here was accepting that marriage brings with it a change of lifestyle. The single life may offer what we believe to be freedom and enjoyment with little responsibility, but this lifestyle is not sustainable in the long-term. Marriage does come with responsibilities and personal sacrifices, but it is a deeper, more fulfilling role and a means of completing half of our deen. This mind-set is broken by acceptance and knowledge of the benefits that marriage can bring.

We also identified the practical barrier of Sheba having to run a household with no knowledge or prior experience. I helped her understand what managing a home entailed, practical advice

---

1   All names in this book have been changed to protect identities but the scenarios are based on actual clients that I have counselled.

on organisational and time management skills, and well as a few cookery tips (much to the delight of her husband!).

Case Study

Sister Noor explained her situation to me, "I have been married for three months and my husband is out most nights with his friends. Every time I approach him to tell him of my dismay he dismisses my feelings and says I am over reacting. I feel that I have no other choice but to leave the marriage."

I told Noor that three months was too short a time to make an informed decision about ending a marriage. I suggested how she could communicate her feelings to her husband effectively and convey to him that his lack of sensitivity was actually causing her to think seriously about ending the marriage. I also invited them to come for counselling as a couple, which, alhamdulillah, they did.

It soon became clear that Brother Kashif was struggling to let go of his single life. He felt he could have it all and eventually his wife would get used to his routine and accept it. He couldn't see why he needed to give up any part of his old life.

I explained that after marriage he had to prioritise and compromise just as his wife was doing. Instead of looking at what he was leaving behind, I urged him to think about what he had to look forward to. Together we came up with a plan that allowed the couple to spend quality time together as well as their individual time with friends and other family.

Although marriage is the merging of two lives, it does not mean that one or both partners need to lose their identity and sense of self. Allah created us in pairs, with different strengths and abilities. When a man and a woman work together within their Allah-given roles while maintaining the characteristics that make each of us unique, then the strength of that partnership is greater than the sum of two individuals working on their own.

Sisters, no matter how highly qualified you are or how successful in your career, once you are married and have children, your main role is as a homemaker. Therefore, it is a good idea to learn homemaking skills and to take pride in caring for your home and family well.

Brothers, your main role is to provide for and protect your family with compassion and affection. Thus, it would be a good idea to secure some means of income. You must also be prepared to give your wife a helping hand with the home and children.

Both partners are responsible for fulfilling each others' spiritual, physical and emotional needs. As you consider what you expect from marriage and what you are able to offer, it is important to consider all these aspects, no matter how mundane they may seem. I have seen many marriages in turmoil due to a difference in opinion about the importance of food and levels of cleanliness.

What to do next:

When you first think about marriage, these are some of the issues that you may wish to consider:

> What are your reasons for getting married? Are you looking for companionship, a soul mate, love, children? Or is it just something you think you are expected to do? The clearer you are about your reasons for getting married, the easier it can be to find someone whose ideas match your own.

- > What do you expect from marriage? Make a list of the things that are essential and the things that would be nice, but you are prepared to compromise on. Refer back to your reasons for getting married as they will influence what you expect. Don't make the list too long!
- > What can you offer a potential spouse? Reflect on your strengths, weaknesses, likes and dislikes with honesty, sincerity and realism.
- > Remember, this is a life change. Single life and married life can never be the same. Accept this and embrace the differences with positivity. Look forward to having someone to share life's journey with.

Even Greater Expectations

In my years of counselling, I have understandably seen more sisters than brothers. I only see brothers within the context of marriage counselling. But before marriage, sisters often tell me that they are looking for their 'perfect' man, to which I always reply, "Only Allah is Perfect."

Case Study

Sister Nadia came to see me as she was frustrated at not being able to find her 'perfect' match despite years of looking. I asked her, "What kind of man do you want to get married to?" Nadia excitedly took her list out of her handbag, handed it to me with a huge smile on her face and said, "I'm not asking for much."

This is what she had written:

» Long beard
» Speaks Arabic
» Attends circles and regularly goes to the masjid
» Does lots of community work
» A professional with a good career and income (because money matters too!)
» Tall and good looking. It's not that important but it would be nice!

Notwithstanding the fact that there are indeed good reasons to have all these attributes, this is what I call choosing 'package over substance'. It all sounds fantastic on the outside, but not much thought has been given to what's on the inside of the package.

I asked Nadia, "Have you thought about whether the potential spouse is kind, caring and potentially a good parent?" Sister Nadia explained, "I assumed he would be all of those things if he has a long beard and attends circles."

Then I asked her, "You haven't mentioned anything on your list about his family background, his upbringing or his past?" To which Nadia replied, "I'm not going to be marrying his family, am I?"

Finally, I asked her whether she wanted her potential husband to spend time at home with her and the children. "Of course!" she exclaimed. I asked her, "Have you thought about where he will get the time to do that if he has a professional career, attends circles and the masjid and is volunteering in the community?!"

We spent a session exploring in detail how Sister Nadia could come up with a list that would be more specific and targeted to her actual needs.

Such mistakes are common and a lot of brothers and sisters come up with lists that sound great but are, in fact, not that well thought out.

It is important to ask yourself what characteristics you are looking for in your spouse and don't assume that appearance, dress or certain actions will guarantee that characteristic. A husband may have a good income, but that does not mean he will automatically be a good provider for you.

Every person is shaped by their past and the people around them. This is why it is important to get an idea of a person's upbringing and whether that means they might bring emotional baggage into the marriage that you need to be prepared for. Even if you are not going to live with them, it is prudent to understand the family that your potential spouse comes from and their values and principles.

This is where parents are a fantastic asset, because at this stage of your life, whether you believe it or not, they probably know you best. They have brought up children themselves, run their homes, cared for their families, handled extended family systems and most importantly, made and learnt from their own mistakes along the way.

I would sincerely recommend that you listen to your parents' advice and learn from the wealth of experience they have gathered. You might think that times have changed and they do not understand your needs or the pressures you face, but I can assure you that your parents will wish the best outcome for you and give you their sincere advice, insha'Allah. Brothers, if your mum knows you love your food, listen to her when she says you won't be happy with a wife who refuses to cook. Sisters, if your mum believes that you are too shy or enjoy your privacy too much to live in an extended family, take heed of that advice.

What to do next:

> Make a check-list of qualities that you feel are essential for your prospective partner to have. Be realistic and practical. This is not a list of ideal qualities as that list could be endless. This is a short check-list of about four or five qualities that are most important to you, that you would not be willing to compromise on.

> Once you have made that short list of essential qualities, you can make a note of aspects that would be nice, but you could live without.

> Be ready to review the list if your life circumstances change, or if for whatever reason, you change your outlook on life.

Physical Attraction

This is a subject that is often surrounded by embarrassment and sometimes not even considered a serious topic of conversation when discussing marriage. Nobody wants to appear shallow when the prospective partner has everything you want, but you're just not attracted to them.

Al-Mugirah ☼ reports that when he got engaged to a woman the Prophet ☼ said, "Look at her for it is more likely to create affection and consent between you both" (at-Tirmidhi). This demonstrates the importance of being physically attracted to a potential spouse.

Thus, I would urge you to consider this aspect honestly when you look at prospective partners. It is not a vain consideration – it is a big part of marriage.

What to do next:

> Be completely honest with yourself. If you believe it is going to be difficult for you to be with someone you're not attracted to, even if they have all the other qualities you are looking for, think very carefully before making a lifelong commitment.

> Do not think any less of yourself for believing this to be important to you. It is better to admit it now than find yourself and your partner in an unhappy relationship years down the line.

Lifestyle and Wealth

Attitudes to money and affluence of lifestyle are also best discussed before marriage. If you are used to a more affluent lifestyle and it is important to you, then there is absolutely no shame in seeking someone who will share that ideal with you. If you choose to marry someone who is not able to provide you with the lifestyle you are accustomed to then you will have to make compromises and adjustments. You need to ask yourself whether you would be prepared to make those compromises without feeling resentful and hard done by.

What to do next:

> Sisters – if you feel that you can only live a certain lifestyle, or there is a minimum standard of living that you expect, then please make that clear before you meet prospective partners.

> Brothers – be honest about your ambitions and finances. If you do not think that you can provide for the prospective partner in the manner that she would like, then please be honest about it

now and save yourself the stress later.

> Sisters and brothers - remember that rizq (provision) is from Allah. Sometimes in life we may have money and Allah ﷻ may test us and take it away from us. If that test happens we should be prepared for it.

Intention with Sincerity *(Ikhlas)*

In Islam, deeds are based upon the intention that precedes them. A successful and healthy marriage should begin with good intentions. So you need to be very honest in answering the question: what are my intentions in getting married?

Of course, we all know that marriage is half of our *deen* and our ultimate goal is to please Allah ﷻ. That almost goes without saying and it would be fantastic if we all had that purity of intention. Nevertheless, the reality is that marriages happen for all sorts of reasons, the noble and the not-so-noble. My experience in marriage counselling has thrown up some rather alarming motives including money, passports and "because I need to get my mum off my back!" You won't be surprised to learn that with intentions such as these, marriages don't have the best of starts. Some of the more common reasons I have heard and my advice regarding them are:

"My family is pressuring me to get married."

We all want to feel loved and accepted within our family and we do what we can to please them. However, it is vital that if you find yourself in this situation, you communicate with them. Perhaps you feel more comfortable relating to someone else who can then communicate your thoughts to your parents. Either way, it is important not to keep quiet. Marriage is a huge undertaking and it should not be entered into with resentment or under pressure.

"My parents think that I am going off the rails and getting married will sort me out."

Some young adults go through rebellious phases or have mental health issues that leave their parents despairing of what to do. There is a worrying mentality among some parents that the solution to these problems is to get their child married. They think that somehow entering into the institution of marriage will be a miraculous cure-all for any 'wild' behaviour and their child will automatically submit to domesticity and cultural norms. Sadly, this doesn't work. The issues that existed before marriage will be carried through into the marriage and cause further problems, this time affecting more lives. Marriage should be entered into by two parties that are ready, willing and mentally and emotionally stable.

"My parents are too strict and I want to move out. Getting married seems like my only option."

When you feel suffocated at home and unable to communicate with your parents, it might seem as though marriage is the ideal solution. However, this is not true. Whatever issues you currently have need to be resolved otherwise you will take them into your married life. Marriage brings its own responsibilities with it and is not the ticket to freedom that you may imagine it to be. The best solution is to talk to your parents or another confidant and come up with a resolution to your issues, so that you can enter into marriage with a healthy attitude.

"I need someone to take over mum's household duties now that she is older." (Brothers)

I have heard this from many brothers who seem to think that their wife will pick up where their mother left off. A number of boys are spoilt by their mothers and, when they grow up into young men, they are unwilling or unable to take on the responsibility of home and family life, or even to look after themselves. They expect a woman (be it their wife or mother) to pick their things up after them, wash their clothes, sort out their paperwork and so on. Brothers, you are marrying a soulmate and companion, not a housekeeper. If you nurture love and affection between you, then of course your wife will gladly carry out her share of the household duties, but be prepared to pull your own weight as well. The best of men, Prophet Muhammad ﷺ, always helped out with the chores.[2]

"I want a fairytale wedding day with my own Prince Charming." (Sisters)

For some sisters it is all about the perfect dress, the ideal setting and that magical honeymoon in the Far East. Instead of concentrating on marriage, these sisters are concentrating on the wedding, the clothes, the jewellery, the attention. To those sisters, I would say you need to look at your priorities. A wedding only lasts a day (or two) but a marriage lasts a lifetime. The fancy clothes and jewellery will be of no use to you if you are not content with your husband.

Every girl dreams about romance and that special someone who will make her feel like a princess all the time. However, this is not a fairytale and we are not the heroines of a 'happy-ever-after' movie. Marriage is a practical business and requires plenty of effort and a level of sacrifice. That is the reality. Of course, there should be love and affection within a marriage, but it is unrealistic to expect a lifetime of hearts and flowers.

---

2   Narrated Aisha, "Allah's messenger ﷺ used to patch his sandals, sew his garment and conduct himself at home as any of you does in his house. He was a human being, searching his garment for lice, milking his sheep and doing his own chores." (at-Tirmidhi)

"I want to marry someone just like my dad." (Sisters)

In the same way that some men want a wife that will pick up where their mothers left off, some girls want a husband to pick up where their father left off. They are so used to being pampered as 'Daddy's little girl' that they are unable to carry out their duties once they are married. This attitude of entitlement will only lead to a marriage full of conflict and unhappiness.

Some sisters also compare the standard of living that their father provided them and want their husband to match it. Sisters, your father has been earning and providing for decades in order to reach the standards that you can enjoy today. Your husband is just starting out, so give him a chance.

What to do next:

> Marriage is not a solution to an existing problem. If you have existing issues, then you will need to resolve these with your family by talking. If you feel that this is difficult for you, ask someone to mediate on your behalf. Don't keep quiet and think that everything will be alright.

> Brothers – Remember that your wife is NOT a replacement for your mum! There are few things more off-putting to a woman than a mummy's boy.

> Sisters – Remember not to compare your husband with your dad. Few husbands will put up with a pampered princess attitude.

> Intention is everything. Your intention should be for the pleasure of Allah and for the safeguarding of your chastity. If your intentions are honourable, then insha'Allah your relationship will be mutually beneficial.

> Desire success. This is a key factor in a healthy marriage. You work hard and strive for the things you desire. So intend to do everything in your power to make your marriage work and provide you both with a lifetime of peace and contentment, insha'Allah.

Are You Ready For This?

We have mentioned that married life is different from single life, but do you know exactly what that means? Have you given any great thought to married life itself or are the wedding preparations more of a priority at the moment? In short, are you ready for this? I put these questions to engaged couples in their pre-marriage counselling and sometimes I get some very strange looks.

Being a spouse will be one of the most important roles in your life and it needs to be thought about and prepared for carefully. By marrying, we are carrying out the Sunnah of the Prophet ﷺ and completing half of our *deen*. Through hadith we know that women can attain their Jannah by their husbands being pleased with them, and that the best of men are those that are best to their wives.[3] So we are not just talking about this life, we are talking about the hereafter as well.

In order to gain these potential rewards, we must be prepared to put in the effort and hard work. This means that brothers and sisters: you must both make a few sacrifices on your time and your personal space in order to accommodate the other. You may have to rein in your anger or forgo an argument and exercise patience in order to keep the peace. I do not mean continuous sacrifice but a level of give-

---

3 Narrated Umm Salamah, "The Messenger of Allah ﷺ said, 'If a woman dies in a state that her husband is pleased with her, she will enter Paradise.'" (at-Tirmidhi) Narrated Abu Huraira, "Allah's Messenger ﷺ said, 'The believers who show the most perfect faith are those who have the best behaviour, and the best of you are those that are best to their wives.'" (at-Tirmidhi)

and-take. You may ask, "Why should I have to sacrifice? Why does it always seem to be me?" I would urge you to think of the rewards and also look at it as a means of personal growth and development.

> *"Mankind!*
> *We created you from a male and female,*
> *and made you into peoples and tribes*
> *so that you might come to know each other.*
> *The noblest among you in Allah's sight is*
> *the one with the most taqwa."*
> (Qur'an 49:13)

People are impatient. They want quick fixes and an easy life with minimal effort. In marriage, as in most other aspects of life, little is achieved except through hard work, and there are few quick and easy answers. We have to constantly work at it. This is what I mean by sacrifice and this is required from both partners right from the start.

It is relatively easier to be giving and sacrificing in the initial honeymoon period, when marriage is still a novelty. Emotions and excitement can take the edge off reality during these first three months. Your spouse's quirky little habits seem endearing and you both want to spend time together, getting to know each other. It is at the three month stage (or thereabouts), when the initial honeymoon period is over, that the realities of life kick in and little things begin to irritate you. This is when the hard work seems to start and, crucially, this is also the time when a number of couples run into problems.

You might wonder why I am mentioning the three month rule in a section about pre-marriage? Well I think it is important at this stage for you to be aware of this phase and to be prepared for it. The first months of marriage are a time of huge change and high-energy emotions. It is fatal to be making rash decisions about the marriage during this time.

Case Study

Sister Noreen had been married for three months, and she noticed that whenever her mother came to visit, her husband pulled a face. In her mind, he was wordlessly expressing his annoyance about her mother's presence. Rather than talking it through rationally and asking him if there was a problem, she took such offence to that, that she asked for a divorce, and sadly for them both, she got it. There was no discussion and thus opportunity to resolve the underlying issues and come to an understanding.

Noreen came back a few years later feeling regretful, but asking me for confirmation of her decision. I told her honestly that it had been too soon after the marriage to make a decision about divorce. A more constructive course of action would have been to communicate her feelings to her husband, acknowledge the validity of his feelings and come to a compromise. Failing, that she could have sought help from her family and/or professional advice. Divorce should be the very last resort when all other avenues have been exhausted, not the first port of call when there is a difference of opinion.

At the other end of the spectrum, I met a couple who thought that they had done plenty of preparation but this was still not enough to prevent tension early on in the marriage.

Case Study

Brother Adeel and Sister Basmah took their commitment to get married very seriously. They went to course after course and learnt all about marriage. They felt they had educated themselves and knew more than enough to approach married life being well aware of each other's rights. They then got married and concentrated on these rights, and indeed in some cases demanded that their own Islamic rights were met. A little while into their marriage, they came to me dissatisfied.

I explained to them firstly, that what makes a successful marriage is not to concentrate on your own rights, but to ensure that you are giving your partner his or her rights. If you have this one rule in place you will see that you automatically receive your rights as well. Secondly, marriage is an institution governed by love and mercy not just a legal contract with a list of boxes to tick. It works best when both parties show understanding and flexibility towards each other and embrace the spirit of being one half of a team.

Adeel and Basmah understood that they had focused too intensely on the contractual details of the marriage and neglected the nurturing side. Once they achieved the balance, they were much more emotionally fulfilled.

What to do next:

> Keep focusing on your intention for marriage. Try to remind yourself daily that you are doing it for the sake of Allah. Hold firmly to this and remember insha'Allah, the benefits to you in this life and the next.

> Be prepared to compromise, adapt and make sacrifices after marriage. A healthy marriage is based on give-and-take.

Let's Be Clear From the Start

By now, you should have a list that contains:
- ✓ the essential aspects that you cannot compromise on
- ✓ the factors that would be nice to have but that you could compromise on
- ✓ what you expect from marriage and your spouse
- ✓ what you can offer

You should also have an essential list of questions that you can ask a potential spouse about practicalities. These should cover location, living arrangements, extended family systems, finances, jobs, attitudes to food, socialising and parenting. It might sound very business-like, but it will save a lot of arguments if these details are ironed out at this stage.

Case Study

Brother Hassan had recently got married. He had a good job and this was one of the reasons Sister Shaheen had married him. One day, he decided on his own to leave his job and start a new business. He came home that evening and announced to his wife what he had done. As you can imagine his wife was shocked that he had done this without discussing it with her first and it caused a lot of conflict.

When they came to see me, I listened to both sides of the story. It was important to Shaheen that her husband had a steady income and the security this provided. Hassan, on the other hand, felt stifled in his job and wanted the flexibility of his own business. But neither party had discussed this prior to marriage and so they had no idea how the other felt. It took many sessions before they were able to reach a solution that they were both comfortable with.

On the other hand, people that have a clear and realistic idea of what they want and communicate effectively with their potential partner are far more likely to be satisfied.

Case Study

Sister Shaheda is knowledgeable in Islam, has two degrees and an excellent job. She got married recently at the age of 33 and people assumed that it was because she was holding out for a similarly educated man with a good profession. In fact, from the start she knew exactly what she was looking for; a kind, caring and considerate person. The man she eventually married had an ordinary job and was not an academic by any means, but as Shaheda confided to me, "He is a real gentleman and he makes me happy." When they have guests, or she is under pressure in her demanding job, he helps to make her life easy. Shaheda was realistic enough to realise that she could not 'have it all' and so she picked the qualities she thought were essential to her and then followed through with this. Alhamdulillah she and her husband are a lovely, happy couple.

What to do next:

> When you communicate with a potential partner, use your list as your guide and keep referring back to it. Make sure that you are satisfied with the answers you have been given to your questions and you are clear about what has been said. Equally, you should make sure that the answers you give are clear.

> Emphasise what is essential to you and make you sure you understand what is essential for your potential partner. A life change, such as leaving your job or deciding you do actually want to continue to live with your parents, may rock your relationship if your partner based their decision to marry you on these points.

Summary

Marriage is a serious and life long commitment to fulfil the emotional, physical and spiritual needs of another person and, in turn, be similarly fulfilled. Before embarking on such an important life phase:

* It is vital to be clear about your intentions for doing so.

* You need to plan and think about what will fulfil you and what you can offer a potential spouse, being realistic and honest about those requirements.

* Accept that married life is very different from single life. Be mentally prepared to make changes and sacrifices in order to make the marriage work.

* Seek advice from your family, who know you best.

❧

Chapter 2

Keeping the Love Alive

Alhamdulillah, you are married. You may be newly married or have been married for a while. Either way there are some golden rules that you can apply to your married life. These apply all the time – not just when you are going through good times or when things are going your way, but day in and day out, every day of your life.

The Three T's of Marriage

Transparency

Right from the moment you meet with a prospective spouse and through every stage of your married life, there should be no secrets or hidden agendas. It is vital that both sides are able to discuss everything with each other, from domestic arrangements to feelings and ambitions openly, honestly and without fear of being mocked or judged. In other words your spouse should be your friend and confidant. Being deceptive, actively lying or covering the truth leads to possessiveness, anxiety and, worst of all, suspicion. Being married means that you are now 'we' and 'us', not 'I' or 'me'. Marriage is about sharing so let transparency be your rule within it.

Trust

When two people are open and honest with each other about all aspects of their lives, then this nurtures a very beautiful quality called trust. Trust gives rise to confidence and contentment within your self and your relationship. However, it is also a delicate thing. It takes constant effort and time to build, nurture and protect trust but only a moment's foolishness to destroy it. Once trust has gone, then it is very difficult to repair the damage. Always be mindful to protect the trust between you and your spouse and to treasure it.

Time

We all spend time on the things we think are important in our lives. So be sincere and generous with the time you give your spouse. It is an investment that will really pay off in your marriage as giving time to your spouse shows them that they and your marriage are important to you. When both husband and wife spend quality time together and give each other their undivided attention, then this promotes communication and harmony. Take time each day to be with each other, catch up with the day's news, tell each other what is on your mind, however trivial, but do make time for each other. It will strengthen your love. By the way, sitting in the same room as your spouse checking Facebook on your device does not count as quality time!

What to do next:

> Be open and honest with your spouse in all matters, regardless of how mundane you think they are. Create a culture in the home where you tell each other everything, perhaps over dinner.

> Trust your spouse completely and do not allow suspicion to enter into your mind. Be mindful that your own behaviour protects the trust that your spouse has in you.

> Spend time together when you can give each other your undivided attention. A little regular time set aside ensures that you stay connected with each other, and promotes transparency and trust.

Courtesy and Manners *(Adaab)*

*"Let whoever believes in Allah and the last day
either speak good, or remain silent."*
(Muslim and al-Bukhari)

Islam pays a great deal of attention to good character and manners. Indeed the Prophet ﷺ personified these in all aspects of his life. It is precisely because of his noble character and exemplary manners that people were drawn to him and loved him. It goes without saying, that as Muslims, we should also strive to emulate that level of courtesy, respect and tolerance in all of our dealings with people, regardless of their background. This applies in equal measure to the strangers that we meet as well as the people that we live with. Unfortunately, we can sometimes slip in our level of conduct with our spouses as familiarity sets in and contempt and carelessness take over.

At home, people often don't think consciously about their manners, tone of speech, use of language, expressions and body language, when in fact, it has a huge impact on the people around us and ultimately on ourselves. As Muslims, we must have a good character and all that it entails, for ourselves and for those around us. The home should be a place of comfort and security for all members of the family. If it becomes as hostile as the outside world, the relationship for the couple, as well as the family, will begin to disintegrate.

We need to be more mindful of our speech and behaviour especially when we are stressed or frustrated. It is all too easy to snap at our spouse when we have had a bad day or simply shut down. However, before we do that we need to think about the consequences. Unnecessary comments, a sharp tone of voice or an ignored kindness can all hurt our spouse a little bit. When it is done over months and years, the hurt builds up and eats away at the love and respect that binds the couple.

So, in practice, what does this mean? It means being kind and gentle; being soft-spoken, not raising your voice, not using crude language or saying hurtful things. If you consistently conduct yourself with good manners and polite and gentle speech, then you will command the love and respect of your spouse and those around you. Even in times of frustration, anger or disagreement, stick to these basic principles and your marriage will flourish. If both husband and wife conduct themselves in this way, it is impossible for a disagreement to descend into a cycle of arguments. You have a cycle of good manners instead!

What to do next:

> Make your intention that from this day forward for the sake of Allah ﷻ, you will try and conduct yourself with excellent manners and speech. What may initially seem like hard work, will soon become second nature, but the effect on your whole life will be remarkable.

> In most successful marriages I have seen, either both or one spouse has a very good character. Try to be that person. It engenders love and your spouse will respect you and listen to you.

> Read the Seerah of the Prophet ﷺ and strive to emulate his example of good character. It was because of this that people were drawn to him ﷺ and insha'Allah, you will find all of your relationships become easier.

Smile!

> *"A smile in your brother's face is charity."*
> (at-Tirmidhi)

We have seen how important good conduct and manners are in creating a calming home environment and a loving marital bond. The first part of this is having a cheerful face. Your spouse will see your face and assess your body language before they hear what you say. So make sure that it is a smile that they see.

A smile can say a hundred things from "I'm glad to have you in my life" to "Yes, I'm willing to compromise". Just that one small action can make the difference between your spouse looking forward to seeing you or not.

Sometimes when the worries of the world are weighing down on our shoulders, it is difficult to raise a smile. However, if you want to have the best possible relationship with your spouse, a harmonious and peaceful home environment and your spouse's undivided attention, then a genuine smile is the best place to start. If you think I am exaggerating, then let me ask you to stand in front of a mirror. First scowl and then smile. Which looks more welcoming, more pleasing to the heart and more beautiful to the eyes?

When I am counselling couples, husbands frequently tell me about their wives, "When I go to work, she's miserable, when I come back, it's the same." This complaint, most of the time, comes from the man. It is rare that I have a woman making the same complaint about her husband. So I would advise sisters, in particular, to let your husband see you smile as he is leaving for work and smiling when he comes back.

Case Study

During a couple's counselling session, Brother Uthman told me that he loved seeing a smile from his wife as he walked through the door. He said, "I don't think she realises but just seeing her smile melts all my troubles away." Consequently, none of his business worries or frustrations are brought into the house, thus creating a more harmonious environment for the family.

What to do next:

> Smile at your spouse before you part ways for the day. This will set the tone for the whole day. You will both have a better start to the day, knowing that you have left the house on a positive note and will hopefully return home to the same.

> Look at yourself in the mirror and see how much better you look, and consequently, how much brighter things can seem when you smile.

> Remember the hadith about a smile being charity. Practising this may well remove any difficulties you may be having, just by giving out that smile! Remember, that you will be earning reward for it and it will become so much easier.

Appreciation

> *"Appreciation can make a day – even change a life.*
> *Your willingness to put it into words is all that is necessary."*
> (Margaret Cousins)

Just as a smile can make someone's day, so too can the simplest acts of appreciation. It is not enough just to be grateful for something in our hearts, we have to put it into words and actions that show the other person that we appreciate them. Everybody likes to be made to feel special; it is part of human nature. When you show appreciation to your spouse, you build their confidence, increase their love for you and fulfil their need to feel special. It sets up the environment for you to receive that same level of fulfilment in return.

Appreciation can take the form of words; a simple "thank you" for doing the washing up or just telling your spouse that you appreciate having them in your life will really make a difference to them. So too can a thoughtful gesture. If your wife has cooked for your parents one day, then offer to make dinner the next. If your husband has come home from work tired then offer to rub his shoulders while dinner is heating up. All these words and gestures build up in the heart and push out any ill feeling there may be.

Case Study

I asked Sister Samia to tell me one of the secrets of her successful marriage. She explained, "I always say jazak Allah to my husband for everything – for taking the rubbish out, giving me a lift, shopping or taking me on holiday. I always make it a point to appreciate everything he does." In doing so, Samia makes her husband feel valued and special, which encourages him to continue doing these thoughtful things. Neither husband nor wife has fallen into the trap of taking each other for granted.

On the subject of appreciation, a frequent complaint I hear from men is, "My wife doesn't cook as well as my mum!" Brothers, please bear in mind that your mum has years of experience of cooking for her family. Give your wife a chance, appreciate whatever she cooks and encourage her. The worst thing you can do is to criticise because it really won't improve the food, and it will make her more prone to giving up. Encouragement and praise brings out the best in all of us, so do your best to show her some appreciation and gratitude when she makes the effort.

On the same note, sisters, please don't compare your husband to your father. Your husband might put up that shelf crooked or hang the wallpaper upside down, but he doesn't have the years of DIY experience that your father has!

What to do next:

> Make a list of the things in your life that your spouse does for you. Don't limit yourself to the big things. Think about all the little things they do that make your life easier or more worthwhile. Don't take anything for granted. Every act of consideration deserves appreciation.

> Plan how you can show your appreciation for these things. It could be a simple "thank you" or running a relaxing bath for your tired spouse.

> Give a daily dose of appreciation.

> In fact, it is worthwhile making a list of things that you appreciate in your life in general. This has an uplifting effect on your whole outlook on life and your level of happiness, which can only benefit all your relationships.

Love and Affection

"Among His Signs is that He created spouses for you of your own kind so that you might find tranquility in them. And He has placed affection and compassion between you. There are certainly Signs in that for people who reflect."
(Qur'an 30:21)

Love is a vital ingredient in marriage. It is what binds the family unit tightly together. Some couples fall in love with each other and then marry. Others marry first and grow to love each other. In both cases, hard work is needed by both spouses to build and maintain the love throughout the marriage. Deep and long-lasting love doesn't strike like lightning. It is constructed like a building. In the first two years (or so), you begin to lay down the foundations for the marriage. The foundation is built on understanding, flexibility, respect, kindness and generosity. Only then can the love be solid.

However, it is not enough for the love to just be present in your heart. You have to show it as affection towards your spouse.

Case Study

Sister Zahra and Brother Kamran came to me for counselling and I asked them what the problem was. Zahra said, "He doesn't love me." Kamran replied, "That's not true. I do love you." Zahra asked, "How do I know that?" To which Kamran responded "Don't I bring you tea in bed every Sunday morning, do I not look after the kids when you're unwell, do I not offer to take them to school when you have loads of work to do?"

We established that Zahra was looking for more obvious statements of love and gestures of affection. When she did not find these within her marriage, she assumed that her husband did not love her. Kamran, on the other hand, was not given to making statements of love and buying flowers and chocolates. He felt that being there for his wife and helping her was more of a practical way of showing his love.

I explained to Kamran that women need to hear words of affection to reassure them of their husbands' love. I also advised Zahra to have a more open-minded view of what a loving gesture could be.

Having love in your heart for your spouse is very important and worthy because indeed Allah ﷻ knows what is in your heart. But it is also incredibly important to express that love with words and actions, otherwise there is the danger that your spouse does not know how you feel and that leads to misunderstanding.

The more you give and show your love and affection, the more you will receive. And perhaps of all of Allah's bountiful blessings to us, surely one of the sweetest is the blessing of loving and being loved completely. It may be that one partner is more demonstrative than the other, one is more comfortable expressing their love than the other, but given time and patience, love will increase between the couple as the years go by.

What to do next:

> Brothers, I kindly remind you that sisters need reassurance of their husband's love regularly and this must be demonstrated with affection. For example, you could refer to her with terms of endearment, express the feelings in your heart and buy her gifts.

> Most people, and especially women, want to be admired, and even after years of marriage still want reassurance that they are desirable. Tell your wife now and again that she looks beautiful, that you have noticed her new dress and you like the way she looks in it. Tell your husband you still find him

handsome and that he looks smart in that jacket. Keep the (genuine) compliments flowing. It is great confidence booster for you both.

> It is very easy for marriage to become just a practical domestic arrangement rather than a loving relationship. It takes hard work and continual effort to keep the love alive. Do not allow your married life to become a series of shouted instructions or constant nagging about housework. Set aside time to talk to each other about your plans, dreams, thoughts and feelings, in fact, anything you want to talk about.

> If it is too difficult to find the time and space at home, book a babysitter if you need to, and go out for a meal together, or just for a walk. Remind each other who you are and why you chose to be together. Re-connect.

> Arrange regular 'date nights' - you are in a halal relationship, so enjoy the time you have together and keep the romance alive. Be husband and wife, appreciate each other in those roles and don't become disengaged as a couple.

Compromise and Sacrifice

There will be times in your married life when you feel like doing something and your spouse feels like doing something different or you both just don't see eye to eye. Instead of arguing about it and allowing something trivial to escalate, the art of compromising and making a little sacrifice goes a long way in saving tears and conflict, and building love and respect.

Case Study

Muhammad has come back late from work after a really bad day. His boss is not pleased because he has not met a deadline, he got stuck in traffic and now he has to work at home to meet the new deadline. He just wants to come home, not speak to anyone, have dinner and shut himself in the study to get on with his work.

Meanwhile, his wife, Sara, has been nursing a sick child, while she has the flu herself. The other children are running around screaming and Sara has just burned the dinner. She wants her husband to come home and take over the child care so that she can go and lie down.

As Muhammad opens the front door, he finds a messy house and rowdy children and the smell of burnt dinner.

Scenario 1: Muhammad storms into the house shouting that he has had a bad day, he's hungry and miserable. He tells off his wife for not having dinner ready or looking after the house and children properly. Sara responds angrily, "You think you've had a bad day. I'm sick, I've spent all day looking after the children and hours in the kitchen only to find that dinner is burnt." And so it becomes an argumentative competition to see whose life is tougher. At the end of the day, Muhammad and Sara are in a bad mood with each other and the children, and dinner has still not been served.

Scenario 2: Muhammad sees that today his wife is struggling because the house and children are not usually in this state. He takes a deep breath, goes into the kitchen and hugs his wife. He spends twenty minutes getting the children to bed, while Sara starts again on dinner. Then he and Sara sit down and talk for a while before he goes and does his work. This scenario results in a much calmer, peaceful evening because both partners have made an effort to do things which they did not feel like doing.

As I have mentioned before, marriage is about 'we' and 'us', not 'I' and 'me'. This means not always concentrating on your own needs. Instead of asking, "What do I want? What am I not getting out of this marriage? Why is it me that always has to do the hard work? Why is it always me who has to say sorry?", you need to start thinking as 'we' and 'us'. You can then rephrase those questions as, "What is best for us? What do we want? How can we move forward together?" These are more constructive questions that allow for resolution.

Case Study

Brother Faisal and Sister Yasmine were very upset with each other when they came to me. Faisal explained that he wanted the family to move to a different area. Yasmine's immediate reaction was to dismiss Faisal's idea because she thought he wanted to be nearer his friends. Every time Faisal would raise the issue, Yasmine would shut him off. They felt that they had reached a dead end because they always ended up arguing and this issue was taking over their lives. Both wanted their own way and neither of them was willing to give in.

During the session, I asked Faisal to explain to Yasmine why he thought this move would be good for the family as a whole. Yasmine realised that Faisal was actually thinking about the children's schooling, his job prospects and her social life. I asked Yasmine to voice her fears and concerns. She said she wanted to be near her parents and parents-in-law in their old age, so that they could take the leading role in caring for them. Surprisingly, neither party had actually communicated these points to each other.

Now they had a clearer understanding of each others' perspective, I encouraged them to go home and ask themselves, "What would be good for us?" and to come back to me a week later.

The following week, they came back looking much happier. Instead of concentrating on themselves as individuals, they had discussed the pros and cons of a move for the whole family. Alhamdulillah, they agreed between themselves to move but not as far as Faisal had originally intended. Both Faisal and Yasmine were happy with this compromise.

It is unhealthy when one partner does all the compromising and sacrificing while the other always gets their own way. Compromise and sacrifice works when both people in a relationship are willing to give and take. In every machine, there is oil to help the moving parts work smoothly. In marriage, it is compromise and sacrifice that help two people to live together harmoniously and for the team to function at its very best.

What to do next:

› The next time a difference of opinion arises between you, try to put yourself in your spouse's position and understand their feelings.

› Instead of having a knee-jerk reaction and dismissing your partner view outright, stop and ask yourself, "What would be the immediate result of allowing my husband/wife to have their way? What would be the long-term effect? What will I gain by digging my heels in? Is there some middle ground that we could both agree upon?"

› Be honest with yourself: Is your need to be right or in control more important than the love between you and your spouse?

› Learn to think as a couple. How are we going to work this out? What can we do?

Appearance

Before marriage and in the early stages, you probably made an effort with your appearance and clothes. Now you're married, you can breathe a sigh of relief and stop worrying about looking your best all the time, right? I'm afraid not. There are so many reasons to love and want to be with a person and these are all wonderful and valid. In fact, it might even sound shallow to be discussing appearance in the same chapter as affection and compromise.

But my years of experience have shown that it's not just that we want to look at somebody who is attractive; we want to know that the other person cares enough to make the effort. Of course, in reality there will be times when you see each other at your worst, and that is also part of the beauty and intimacy of marriage, but these times should be compensated by periods in which we make the effort to look our best for our partner.

Abu Huraira narrated that it was said to the Messenger of Allah ﷺ, "Which of the women is best?" He replied, "The one who makes her husband happy when he looks at her..." (an-Nasa'i). Of course, brothers, you shouldn't neglect yourselves either. Whilst it is often thought that physical attraction is more important to men than women, it doesn't let you off the hook. Let your wife know you care enough about her by trying to look your best too.

Case Study

Brother Noman explained to me that his wife refuses to make an effort with her appearance even though he had mentioned it several times. "When I come home from work, she has the same clothes as she had on in the morning and sometimes she hasn't even combed her hair." As a consequence of this he was considering separating from her. I asked his wife, Sister Nazneen, what was preventing her from abiding by his wishes. She explained that she had three children and was tired and overwhelmed by all the housework and childcare. "When do I get the time to think about myself?"

Both Noman and Nazneen had valid points. I asked Noman what he felt he could do to give his wife the time to concentrate on herself. He said that he could look after the children and do the dishes in the evening.

I saw them both a few months later, and alhamdulillah they implemented these suggestions and now both of them are much happier.

The above case illustrates a simple fact that we sometimes ignore, namely that when you want something from your spouse, you should try to create the environment to make it possible. The above case study is typical of the complaints I hear about appearance, although the advice applies equally to men.

I actually run a separate self-care workshop, because this issue is so prevalent in many of the marriage problems I have to address today. So my advice to brothers and especially sisters: Look after yourself; build your relationship with yourself and with Allah ﷻ. If you do not want to do it for anyone else, do it for yourself and your sense of self worth.

What to do next:

> Factor in some time every day to take care of your appearance.
> Make an effort to make the best of yourself, for your own sake as well as your spouse.
> Look in the mirror. If you're not entirely happy with your state of attire, then it is unlikely that your spouse will be either.

The Three C's of Harmony

I wanted to close this chapter with something that I talk about in my workshops. These are what I call, the 'Three C's of Harmony', which can make a huge difference to marriage when followed.

Consideration

Consideration means putting other people first, taking care of their needs before your own. It is the opposite of being selfish and demanding. In the context of marriage, it means being thoughtful and sensitive towards your spouse, thinking about what they need or feel rather than what you want.

For example, if your wife has been up all night with the baby, offer to look after the baby for a couple of hours so that she can get some sleep. Undoubtedly, that is what she needs and if you are able to, then you should make every effort to try and fulfil that legitimate need. It shows that you are thinking about her and care about her well-being.

Your husband wants to go to the biggest football game of the season, but it clashes with your parents coming to dinner. Consider the following: could you change dinner with your parents to another day? Could you go ahead without your husband and he can join you later? This is the kind of consideration for your husband which will reap rewards because you have considered his needs and wants.

Consideration is caring and kindness in action and is one of the most important things in any relationship. It shows that you care, that you want to make things harmonious and your commitment in making these gestures shows that you don't always put yourself first.

What to do next:

> Think about your partner's needs; are they worried or stressed at work? How is a particular situation affecting them? What care and consideration could you show that would help them right now? Perhaps you could give them a smile, a reassuring hug, or just not pile more problems on them at the moment.

> Walk in each other's shoes. Put yourself in your partner's place. If you were in their situation, what would you want them to do for you?

> Give to receive. Giving is infectious. You will find that the more consideration you give, the more you will receive.

> It's a two way street. When both people consider each other's needs first, there can be no losers.

Co-operation

Co-operation can be defined as listening, engaging, discussing and working towards a common solution. When a problem or issue first raises itself within the marriage, listen to what the other person is saying and do not dismiss it. Voice your own concerns frankly and openly and listen carefully to the response you receive. Look at the positives and negatives of the situation. Persevere and keep your calm. Slowly but surely, like untangling a ball of wool, you will get there in the end.

For example, you want to take a mountain climbing holiday while your spouse just wants a relaxing break. A compromise could be to take two shorter breaks, or to settle on a holiday which combines the two.

Put simply: co-operation is to **listen, acknowledge, reflect, accept** and then **discuss**. And remember to always keep **cool, calm** and **collected**.

What to do next:

> Don't dismiss your partner's ideas without hearing them first.
> Find uninterrupted time and space to sit down and calmly talk through the problem or difficulty that you are facing, without judgement on either side.
> If you find yourself going round in circles and not moving forward, then take a break and come back a bit later.
> A successful solution is not about winning or point-scoring, it is

about working together to achieve the best solution possible for everyone concerned.

Care and Concern

Care is a virtue that is strongly encouraged in Islam; care for parents and children are particularly rewarded. We know that the Prophet ﷺ, was often concerned when, for example, someone was missing from the masjid at prayer time. It is not only care for people that is encouraged, but also for animals and the earth itself. So these are attributes that we should certainly be working on all the time.

With regards to marriage, care and concern for your spouse are bedrocks of your relationship. But to make any meaningful difference, they have to be practiced regularly and indeed become habitual. Showing concern and care means different things to different people and depends on your partner. So part of this trait is to be in tune with your spouse's needs and what will make them happy.

During a particularly hectic and stressful period, try to work out what would mean more to your spouse. Would they prefer a hug and reassurance or would they appreciate practical help, like washing the dishes?

The mark of a strong relationship is where each partner is in tune with the others' needs and knows how and when to show care and concern without being asked.

What to do next:

> Whatever is important to your wife/husband should be important to you. Make their needs your priority.
> What is needed at all times, but particularly at stressful or

difficult times, is to find out what is needed, right here, right now. What can I do to make my partner's life easier?

> Marriage is about fulfilment of needs, and showing care and concern demonstrates that you are committed to fulfilling your spouse's needs naturally and without always being reminded.

Summary

In this chapter, we have looked at the key tools that we need to maintain our marriages and make them into successful and mutually beneficial ventures for ourselves and our partners in this life and the next. It is not one or two of these aspects that will make the marriage a success in a short space of time but the continual application of ALL of these things that will insha'Allah build a strong and long-lasting marriage. In order to keep your marriage strong and the love alive:

* Refer back to your intention and keep referring back!

* Recap on your reasons for marriage. Think about the longevity of your marriage, not just the here and now.

* Remember, we are on a journey; it's not about achieving everything in this life, it's about the next life.

* Replace the 'I' and 'me' with 'us' and 'we'.

Chapter 3

❧❦❧

Reflecting on 'Me' to Improve 'Us'

A number of the couples that come to me for counselling because of problems in their marriage, are armed with a long list (sometimes literally!) of complaints about their partner. It is rare, though, for one partner to be the cause of all the problems. I give these couples the same basic advice and that is: to reflect and work on their own personal behaviour and pave the way to bring out the best in the other partner. Whatever qualities you would like to see in your partner, you will have to cultivate them in yourself first and the rest will, insha'Allah, follow.

In the light of my experience, I feel that the following are the most important qualities and behaviours to work on. However, simple or irrelevant they may seem to your particular problem or circumstances, I assure that you that by implementing these in your life, you will insha'Allah see huge positive changes, both personally and within your marriage.

Surrendering to Allah's Roles

"Men have charge of women because Allah has preferred the one above the other and because they spend their wealth on them. Right-acting women are obedient, safeguarding their husbands' interests in their absence as Allah has guarded them."
(Qur'an 4:34)

There are many books you can buy and courses you can attend that will give you all the information you need about your marital roles, rights and responsibilities and therefore I am not going to cover them here. What I will say is that Allah has created men and women with different strengths and skills and given them specific roles to play in marriage. When men assume the role of provider and protector and women look after their home and family, then they complement each other and the result is, insha'Allah, a well-run home and family with material possessions as well as the love that only a woman can provide.

Society however, tells us that we can compete in these roles and indeed, do them better than each other. So when women decide they can provide for their families too, it is hardly surprising that men expect them to assume that role as well. This 'double burden' is now very common in households, where women work but must also be the nurturer, cook, cleaner and teacher to name just a few responsibilities. This leaves them exhausted and frustrated and causes tension within the marriage.

Allah did not give men and women identical roles but complementary ones. Each partner should be given respect for their role in the relationship and each role is equally as important. The wife/mother role is nurturing, providing love and affection, supporting family members. This complements the husband who is the provider, protector, the guardian from the external environment.

Before you go over the finer details of your role and the rights due to you, you need to understand and embrace the concept of surrendering to these Allah-given roles. This means, as in everything in your life, placing your focus on what Allah ﷻ has asked of you, and surrendering to it, because as our Creator, He knows best. Embrace your roles in the marriage for His pleasure. Look at your own obligations, are you fulfilling them? This will lead to kindness, mercy and respect for one another. As a result, half the work is done in marriage.

Sadly, some people choose to concentrate on receiving their rights and use them as a stick with which to beat their spouse, without looking to what their responsibilities are.

Case Study

Sister Aishah came to me at her wit's end. Her husband was most insistent that she be obedient to him. However, where her rights were concerned, he most definitely wasn't fulfilling them. He was failing to provide financially for the family, was out all the time and was addicted to gambling. In spite of this, he believed that it was her duty as a Muslim wife to be obedient to him and his motto was, "Whatever I say, goes."

One day, she went to give the children something to eat only to realise that the cupboards and fridge were bare and she snapped, finally aware that this wasn't right for her or for the children. When her husband returned home, she took his debit card from him and asked "How can I be obedient to somebody who is disobedient to the creator?"

As you can imagine, this realisation was a turning point for the family and they both came to me for counselling. I explained to them that in order for partners to respect each other, they must both fulfil their basic duties.

On the other hand, when two people surrender to the will of Allah for His pleasure, then insha'Allah not only do they earn that pleasure but they are also blessed with a stable marriage.

Case Study

Sister Hiba was very well educated with a good job and was looking for a husband. A friend told her about a family friend of her brother's who had been looking for a spouse for some time, but because of his ethnicity, he was having difficulty finding someone. On finding out more about the good character of the brother, Hiba asked to be introduced and alhamdulillah, they decided to get married within weeks. Before the marriage, each of them made clear what they could offer to the marriage and what they wanted. Abdul Bari was very clear in telling Hiba that he wasn't well off, and neither was he money oriented so they were never likely to have a luxurious lifestyle and Hiba accepted this. He also told her that family and marriage were his priority and so he would prefer her to concentrate on being a home maker in the future.

After the marriage, Hiba voluntarily offered to buy some comforts for their marital home as she saw that her husband was struggling and she had a well-paid job.

A few years later, Abdul Bari requested that Hiba stop working so that they could concentrate on their marriage and having a family. Again, Hiba did not object as this had been mutually agreed before the marriage.

Now on the face of it, it may sound to you as if Hiba made all the sacrifices. However, she entered marriage with the purest of intentions. She did not care about looks, ethnicity or a high standard of living. She focused on good character and a family minded man. Furthermore, both partners were open and honest with each right from the start, so they both had clear and realistic expectations of each other and both fulfilled these with compassion and flexibility.

Once they had decided to start a family, Hiba and Abdul Bari surrendered to their natural roles and through this gained such a level of inner peace and satisfaction in their marriage that it was a pleasure to be in their company.

This case shows that surrendering to Allah's roles does not mean that a woman should not be educated or work. However, her priority should be her home and family. Brothers and sisters, know your roles and the rewards for fulfilling them. Submit to them and it will bring you peace and happiness.

What to do next:

> Be comfortable in the roles which Allah ﷻ has ordained for you. Remember there are rewards for submitting to those roles and insha'Allah, peace and happiness will be the result.

> Concentrate on your own role and obligations; focusing on how and to what extent you are fulfilling it, rather than concentrating solely on the rights that you are not receiving.

> Remember that you are a male and a female. Try not to compete with each other in those roles. Instead help each other in your respective roles, by supporting, enriching and advising.

> If you need to advise your spouse, be attentive as to how you do this and approach the task with patience and kindness.

Are We Really Married?

As a practical religion, Islam has outlined what our obligations and duties are towards our spouse. However, marriage is more than just about fulfilling legal obligations and duties towards our partners. It is about embracing the concept of being a couple and wanting for our partners what we would want for ourselves.

When one or both partners are not treating each other with the same principles as they apply to themselves, it creates a distance between husband and wife that only gets wider with time as each partner perpetuates a cycle of withdrawing and holding back.

Case Study

Sister Ameera came to me with her husband, Brother Sajid. She explained that they had been married for five years. At the beginning of the marriage, she stayed at home and Sajid was the breadwinner. He paid the rent and the household bills and expenses. However, he never gave her any money for things like clothes, cosmetics and extras that she would like to buy for herself. This was not because he was short of money, as he did spend money on comforts for himself.

Ameera started to do a part-time job, with her husband's permission so that she could save up some money and spend on basic clothes and accessories for herself. After a while, Sajid started asking her to pay one or two of the household bills as well. She told me, "I don't really feel like I am cherished in this marriage."

Sajid felt that he was fulfilling his obligations by providing food and accommodation for his wife. Once she had started to work, he said she spent less time in the home and so it was only fair that she contribute to the household expenses.

I explained to them both that marriage is a partnership in which each party shares whatever they have with each other generously and without holding back. That applies to money, time, affection, effort and so on. I explained to Sajid that he should spend generously of his income on his wife in order to earn her love and affection. After all the Prophet ﷺ said to Sa'd ibn Abi Waqas, "Know that you will never spend anything seeking thereby the Countenance of Allah, but you will be rewarded for it, even (the food) that you put in your wife's mouth"(al-Bukhari). I explained to Ameera that now she knew what her rights were, she should not hesitate to ask respectfully that they be fulfilled.

Case Study

Brother Rehan brought his wife, Sister Parveen, to counselling. "I work really hard to fulfil my duty to provide for my family. I spend generously on my wife and buy her whatever she asks me to. I have provided her with a cleaner and gardener to make her household duties easier, but she is always asking for more. I feel like this is a one way street."

Parveen said, "It is my husband's duty to provide for me. I'm only asking for my rights."

I explained to the couple that there was an imbalance in the marriage. Rehan was working as hard as he could to provide generously for his wife, often at the expense of his own free time, while Parveen was focusing more on her convenience and comfort. It was not clear to Rehan what efforts Parveen was making while he was busy earning. This was beginning to turn into resentment for his wife.

I asked Parveen to come up with a list of the expenses that she felt she needed from her husband and those she could live without, while being mindful of reducing the burden on her husband. I also encouraged Parveen to be generous with her time and efforts towards her husband, so that the balance in their relationship could be restored.

What to do next:

> Marriage is about giving of yourself to another person completely and sharing whatever you have with them generously.

> Brothers - be generous with your income and spend on your wife as you spend on yourself. Share your time and effort in helping her with household chores.

> Sisters - protect and look after whatever your husband has given you and be mindful of not burdening him. Be generous with your time and efforts towards your husband. Of course, it is his responsibility to provide for you. However, if there are times that he is struggling then perhaps you could help by doing without something in order to relieve his stress.

Recognising the Differences

"Live together with them correctly and courteously.
If you dislike them, it may well be that you dislike
something in which Allah has placed a lot of good."
(Qur'an 4:19)

Allah ﷻ has created men and women to complement each other; we are equal but different in the way our brains work. Women tend to be emotional whereas men are very good at hiding their feelings. At best, these two qualities work to balance each other out thus creating a harmonious relationship. However, these differences can also be the cause of misunderstanding and conflict.

Sisters often complain to me, "I can't connect emotionally with my husband" or "He doesn't care about me". Men hide their feelings and ignore them rather than confronting them. So when they are faced with their feelings, they will shut down and withdraw. Women interpret this as a lack of love or an absence of connection.

Brothers often complain that their wives repeat themselves, nag, raise their voices and treat them disrespectfully. Women are much more forthcoming and need to give voice to their concerns, anxieties and fears as soon as they arise. They want to have a conversation with someone, preferably now! When they find that their husband has shut down, they get increasingly agitated and raise their voice. This only serves to shut down the husband even more and so the cycle continues.

When we recognise that men and women are hard-wired differently, then we can take the first step towards a resolution.

Sisters – A man's primary need is for respect. Always communicate respectfully to your husband. If you feel that your emotions are getting the better of you, then remove yourself from the situation. Do *wudu,* do ten sit ups, do anything else that will calm you down or get those pent up feelings out of your system. Respect is not only about the words you use, it is also about the tone of voice you employ and your body language. Men are visual creatures and they find rude body language more offensive than the actual words. So please try not to point a finger at him as if you are talking to a child or stand over him with your hands on your hips. Sometimes it isn't about what you say but how you say it. Respecting your husband means respecting his wishes, his advice and his decisions (as long as they do not go against the wishes of Allah).

Brothers – I have heard from you all so many times telling me that you just don't understand what women want! So, I am going to tell you. A woman's primary need is for love. They just want validation, affection, kindness, and sometimes, they just want to hear a compliment. One of the worst things that you can do is to just ignore your wife and walk away when she is talking to you.

This is a reciprocal cycle. The more respect a woman shows her husband, the more ground she will gain on love.

Case Study

This is a typical scenario in almost every household. The wife has been at home looking after the children all day. She has lots of thoughts and things to say but she has no-one to say them to during the day. When the husband comes home, she can't wait to start talking to him, but he has had a hard day at work and doesn't feel like talking to anyone. His first thought is, "Oh no! I don't want to hear it right now. I can't deal with this."

She begins to talk. He ignores her. She sits and seethes that he never pays any attention to her needs. For some reason, it is like the husband doesn't want to acknowledge his wife's feelings and that just makes her mad and she just wants to scream and shout. Of course, then her husband says that she is being disrespectful. When this happens day in and day out, then it builds tension and resentment in the house.

Both parties have valid points of view. The wife hasn't had adult conversation all day and so wants to talk to her husband. The husband has been dealing with people and problems all day long and does not want to come back home to this.

The solution is for the wife to wait until the husband is relaxed and receptive to hearing what she has to say.

What to do next:

> Make an effort to understand the differences between you. That will help you to understand why the other behaves the way they do, what they need and how you can help fulfil that need.

> Sisters - wait for a good time to speak to your husband, when he is relaxed and doesn't have other stresses on his mind. You will receive a better response in the long run.

> Brothers - don't always try and solve her problems. She doesn't always want you to solve them. Sometimes you just need to validate her feelings by saying, "OK that must have been hard." It would also help if you said, "Do you want to talk about it?" but when you're both ready.

Communication

One of the surprising things that comes up time after time in my marriage counselling sessions is the wife will say, "Why didn't he know what I was thinking? I was upset. Didn't he see me crying, didn't he notice my facial expressions?"

Well this may come as a shock to you, sisters – men can't read minds (or, it seems, facial expressions for that matter)! They don't know unless you tell them. This is one of the differences between men and women. Women sense emotions, see facial expressions, hear the tone of a voice and we can very quickly assess the situation and gauge someone's mood. Men need to be told. I repeat, if you want something or you want them to know about something then tell them!

I repeat this a lot when I'm doing my marriage counselling. When sisters tell me their needs are not being met, I ask them, "Did you ask him? Did you tell him this is how you were feeling?" To which every single sister replies, "He should have known." Husbands are always telling me, "She didn't tell me that it was important to her. I didn't know she felt that way."

Sisters, learn this lesson and learn it well – your husband can't read your mind. So, let us try to make life simpler and actually talk to each other.

Case Study

I was waiting for Sister Asma who was running very late for her appointment. When she arrived, she told me that she had asked her husband to give her a lift and look after the baby while she was with me, and they had agreed it the night before. However, when she woke up in the morning, he was still sleeping. She tried to wake him once, then just got herself and the baby ready and travelled on two buses to get to me. I asked her why she didn't try harder to wake her husband up, not in an aggressive way, just asking him nicely to get ready. Her reply was, "He should have known. I can't keep asking him."

Case Study

Sister Yusra does a huge amount of work in the house and yet her husband asks her to do even more, pay bills, manage the household finances. She is overwhelmed by the amount of work that she has to do. I asked her if she had told him how she feels and explained how much she has to do. Once again, the reply was "Doesn't he see? He should know."

My advice to both of these ladies was the same, "If you don't ask you don't get. Don't blame your husband if he doesn't do something you haven't asked him to!"

Communication isn't just about the words we use. Research has shown that when people are communicating feelings and attitudes, only 7% of the message is conveyed by words, 38% is the tone of those words and 55% the body language. This is something we should be aware of when we are communicating with our spouses. We must ensure that we are making our point (not just ranting), in an even and soft-spoken tone of voice using non-aggressive body language. This will ensure the best possible response from your spouse.

Case Study

A wife has served dinner to her husband. When he has finished, he gets up from the kitchen table and goes to watch TV.

Scenario 1: The wife storms over to the living room with one hand on her hip and the other hand pointing a finger at her husband. She starts shouting about how he takes her for granted and never cleans up after himself and leaves plates and clothes lying around for her to pick up. "Who do you think I am? Your wife or your servant?" she shouts, still waggling that finger.

Scenario 2: The wife walks into the living room and calmly, with a smiling face simply asks her husband to please put his plate in the dishwasher.

You can imagine which scenario ends with an argument and which one results in the wife's request being met.

Effective communication is a process that involves two people and so it is equally important that the listener is as aware as the speaker. When your spouse is talking to you, you need to listen, and most importantly, to hear what they are saying. That means taking on board what they are saying and responding appropriately. Turn your body towards your spouse, make eye contact and use body language, such as nodding, to show that you are listening to what they are saying.

Communication in a marriage is different from a meeting at work in that there are emotions involved. Neither partner should dismiss the other's feelings. Denying your partner's feelings negates their need for speaking out and for healing. When you respond to your partner telling you their feelings, start by validating those feelings. Men, in particular, are guilty of launching into a problem solving exercise when all your wife wants to hear is that you understand.

If your wife was late getting the children to school this morning because she didn't get up on time, she will not appreciate being told to set the alarm clock earlier for the next day. She already knows to do that. She wants you to understand that maybe she couldn't get up on time because she was waiting up late for you to come home or looking after a baby all night.

Take some time to process all the information that you are presented with – your spouse's words, their tone, their body language, any underlying issues and stresses that you think may be present in their life.

What to do next:

> Talk to each other. If you want your spouse to know something, you have to tell them directly.

> Take the time to listen to each other. However irrational it may seem to you, your spouse's feelings need to be expressed and heard.

> Remember the three factors that are important in communication:

- Time: you will learn the best time to communicate with your spouse as you get to know them better. For example when your husband comes home from work may not be the right time; however, after dinner may be a better time.

- Choose your words carefully. You are more likely to engage the other person's attention if you are speaking rationally, to the point and in a soft tone of voice.

- Body language: this should be in harmony with your words. Be relaxed and do not assume aggressive and threatening actions.

> D-day. Have a mutually agreed upon day of communication say, once a month, where the two of you will sit down without interruptions and discuss anything you want. This has been one of the most successful techniques that I have shared with my couples. It ensures that the wife has her husband's undivided attention at least once a month, so she does not have to keep trying to collar his attention at times that are inconvenient for him. He knows that there is a specific time for talking, so he does not have to be forthcoming all the time. Don't just use this time to voice concerns and complaints,

otherwise neither of your will look forward to this window of communication. Use it to discuss more positive topics as well, such as what your goals and achievements are or how grateful you are to have each other.

Forgive and Forget, Overlook and Ignore

It is important in any relationship, but especially in marriage to ignore and overlook, forgive and forget. Marriage is not always plain sailing and loving exchanges. There will be disagreements, times when we are hurt or just unhappy about the way we have been spoken to or treated. So how do we get through these times and back to a state where we are content within the marriage? Well, this is all comes back to your intention for getting married and maintaining it according to the principles we covered in Chapter 2. You need to sacrifice your immediate and relatively minor need for arguing back against the greater good of maintaining marital harmony and acting to seek Allah's pleasure.

** At this point I need to make explicitly clear that I am talking about the minor disagreements that couples have periodically, the occasional insensitive comments and lazy behaviour that leads to hurt feelings and bruised egos. I should stress that domestic violence, mental or emotional abuse or oppression are not issues that should be overlooked or 'put up with'. **

A man said to Imam Ahmed, "A state of well-being is achieved through ten things, and nine of them are overlooking people's faults." Imam Ahmed then said, "Rather a state of well-being is achieved through ten things, and ALL of them are overlooking people's faults."[4]

What does this mean for us? Essentially, it means that unless we can overlook each other's faults, it will be very difficult to find our own contentment. By not letting go of small matters, we not only cause anxiety and resentment within ourselves, we create a cycle of petty behaviour within the marriage that will only escalate with time. So when those rocky patches do occur, our first thought should be to overlook and make excuses for our partner.

Case Study

Your husband comes home in a grumpy mood. He just snaps a few words at you before shutting himself away in the living room in front of the TV. You have spent a good few hours making sure that the house was clean and the meal was appetising. You feel unappreciated and taken for granted.

Your first thought might be to either barge into the living room and sternly tell your husband that he always takes you for granted or sulk and resolve not to spend so much time cooking for your husband the next day. If you do that then you will continue a cycle of petty retaliating behaviour. Small irritations get blown out of proportion and end up in huge long running arguments.

You could on the other, stop and think. Make excuses. Perhaps he has had a bad day or maybe something is weighing on his mind

---

4 *Ghidha' al-Albab Sharh Manzumat al-Adab* by Imam Muhammad al-Saffarini

from work. You could go into the living room and squeeze his hand and then leave him to have his space. This way, you have diffused the situation, shown your maturity and strength of character. It may not be appreciated immediately but it will certainly leave a positive mark in your husband's mind.

Similarly, husbands, make excuses for your wife when her words or behaviour are not up to their usual high standards. Give her a hug, ask her if she needs to talk or offer to do something for her so she can have half an hour of me-time.

Islam values and advocates forgiveness. In fact it is absolutely essential in maintaining relationships between people, not least husband and wife. Allah ﷻ advises us in the Qur'an:

"Make allowances for people, command what is right,
and turn away from the ignorant."
(Qur'an 7:199)

"They should rather pardon and overlook.
Would you not love for Allah to forgive you?"
(Qur'an 24:22)

So if we forgive others for the sake of Allah, we hope that Allah will forgive our sins and show mercy to us and we are all in need of His forgiveness and His mercy.

If:
· You're having to make excuses on behalf of your spouse on a continual basis;
· You are struggling to meet their expectations;

- You feel that resentment is building up inside and you find it hard to let go;
- You find it hard to forgive and move on;

then this is time to seek counselling so that these deep seated issues can be resolved within a professional and non-judgmental setting.

What to do next:

> In cases of small mistakes, make excuses for one another.

> Ignore the small arguments and irritations and overlook them. Do not continue the cycle of bickering and petty behaviour for the sake of your own ego. Rather diffuse the situation and end the cycle because this is the more noble path to take.

> Practice the art of forgiveness. If this seems hard, then think how you would like Allah ﷻ to forgive you when you have made a mistake.

> Even though you may have forgiven, it is hard to forget when you have been hurt. However, forgiveness comes hand in hand with forgetting. This means you must resist the temptation to bring up the problem in every future argument.

Patience (Sabr)

Patience (*Sabr*) is one of the foremost qualities required of a Muslim. The attribute of patience is mentioned many, many times in the Qur'an, as is the reward.

> *"Those who patiently persevere will truly receive a reward without measure!"* (Qur'an 39:10)

This command to be patient applies to all aspects of our life from being stuck in traffic, to family difficulties through to bereavement. It is not fitting for a believer to fall into despair or to be devoid of hope, rather he should always have faith in Allah's mercy. A beautiful analogy of a patient Muslim can be found in the hadith:

> Narrated by Abu Huraira that Allah's Messenger ﷺ said, *"The example of a believer is that of a fresh tender plant; from whatever direction the wind comes, it bends it, but when the wind becomes quiet, it becomes straight again. Similarly, a believer is afflicted with calamities (but he remains patient till Allah removes his difficulties.) And an impious wicked person is like a pine tree which keeps hard and straight till Allah cuts (breaks) it down when He wishes."* (al-Bukhari)

In other words, "those who do not bend, break", and this is often the case when arrogance or a stubborn attitude has crept in. Again, I would like to make the distinction as to when it is correct to have patience and when it isn't. Patience does not extend to putting up with domestic violence, mental or emotional abuse or oppression. These issues are simply too serious to be dealt with simply by being patient and neither is it within our religion to do so. What I am referring to is patience in everyday matters.

Allah ﷻ tells us in the Qur'an that we will be tested with fear, hunger, loss of possessions, livelihood and wealth.[5] We will also be tested by our spouses and children.[6] So we should not expect that life will be plain sailing, rather we should look towards how we can steer ourselves through these storms. Remember, all phases in our lives, good and bad, are temporary and will pass.

---

5 Qur'an 2:15
6 Qur'an 64:14

Case Study

To illustrate the importance of patience, I have taken this 'case study' from the hadith. It is the story of Prophet Ibrahim ﷺ and his son, Prophet Isma'il ﷺ, which has much to teach us in this regard.

Ibn Abbas narrated that the Prophet ﷺ said, "... After Isma'il's ﷺ mother had died, Ibrahim ﷺ came after Isma'il's ﷺ marriage in order to see his family that he had left before, but he did not find Isma'il ﷺ there. When he asked Isma'il's ﷺ wife about him, she replied, 'He has gone in search of our livelihood.' Then he asked her about their way of living and their condition, and she replied, 'We are living in misery; we are living in hardship and destitution,' complaining to him. He said, 'When your husband returns, convey my salutation to him and tell him to change the threshold of the gate (of his house).' When Isma'il ﷺ came, he seemed to have felt something unusual, so he asked his wife, 'Has anyone visited you?' She replied, 'Yes, an old man of so-and-so description came and asked me about you and I informed him, and he asked about our state of living, and I told him that we were living in a hardship and poverty.' On that Isma'il ﷺ said, 'Did he advise you anything?' She replied, 'Yes, he told me to convey his salutation to you and to tell you to change the threshold of your gate.' Isma'il ﷺ said, 'It was my father, and he has ordered me to divorce you. Go back to your family.' So, Isma'il ﷺ divorced her and married another woman from amongst them (i.e. Jurhum).

Then Ibrahim ﷺ stayed away from them for a period as long as Allah wished and called on them again but did not find Isma'il ﷺ. So he came to Isma'il's ﷺ wife and asked her about Isma'il ﷺ. She said, 'He has gone in search of our livelihood.' Ibrahim ﷺ asked her, 'How are you getting on?' asking her about their sustenance and living. She replied, 'We are prosperous and well-off (i.e. we have everything in abundance).' Then she thanked Allah. Ibrahim ﷺ said, 'What kind of food do you eat?' She said, 'Meat.' He said, 'What do you drink?' She said, 'Water.' He said, 'O Allah! Bless their meat and water.' ... Then Ibrahim ﷺ said to Isma'il's ﷺ wife, 'When your husband comes, give my regards to him and tell him that he should keep firm the threshold of his gate.' When Isma'il ﷺ came back, he asked his wife, 'Did anyone call on you?' She replied, 'Yes, a good-looking old man came to me,' so she praised him and added, 'He asked about you, and I informed him, and he asked about our livelihood and I told him that we were in a good condition.' Isma'il ﷺ asked her, 'Did he give you any piece of advice?' She said, 'Yes, he told me to give his regards to you and ordered that you should keep firm the threshold of your gate.' On that Isma'il ﷺ said, 'It was my father, and you are the threshold of the gate. He has ordered me to keep you with me.'" (al-Bukhari)

Isma'il's ﷺ first wife complained to an apparent stranger about her hard living conditions. On hearing this, Ibrahim ﷺ asked his son to divorce her. This was because his daughter-in-law did not display patience and so he felt that she would not make a fitting and supportive wife and mother to a prophet.

Isma'il's ﷺ second wife, on the other hand, praised Allah for whatever she had and showed patience, gratitude to Allah and support for her husband. Ibrahim ﷺ felt these were good qualities for his daughter-in-law to have and so he signalled his blessing to the couple.

What to do next:

Being patient means:

> Calmly accepting the will of Allah
> Refraining from despair and panic
> Not complaining to other people, rather complaining only to Allah as the Prophets (peace be upon them) did when they were afflicted with a trial
> Not blaming others for your predicament or wondering "what if?"
> Not abandoning the principles of the Qur'an and Sunnah
> Actively seeking Allah's help through increased worship[7]

Gratitude: Which of your Lord's favours will you deny?

"If you are grateful, I will certainly give you increase"
(Qur'an 14:7)

The counterpart of patience is gratitude. There is an inexhaustible list of things that we can be grateful to Allah ﷻ for and there can truly never be enough gratitude. Gratitude can be for the simple fact that we can get out of bed every day or smell a rose or hear birdsong.

We often focus on what we don't have in our lives or on our problems. In doing so, we see them as bigger issues than they actually are. Being grateful and focusing on what we have been blessed with puts our problems and our own situations into perspective. In turn, this has an amazingly positive impact on the way we look at life and our relationships. Situations and difficulties that once seemed insurmountable no longer seem so bad.

---

7 See al-Jawziyah's *'Uddat as-Sabirin was dhakirat ash-Shakirin* (Patience and Gratitude)

One of the wisdoms in Islam is to look to the less fortunate so that we can be grateful for what we have.[8] Similarly, Allah has explained to us that the situation of the believer is always good. When a good thing occurs, he says "Alhamdulillah", and likewise when bad happens, he says "Alhamdulillah".[9] By following these simple teachings, we can change our perspective on everything.

To those women who are married, think of those sisters who pray every night for a pious spouse and yet are still single. To those men who have jobs, think of those that are struggling to provide for their families. To those couples who have children, you have no idea what a childless couple would give to be in your place. To those of us who have a roof over our head, a meal on our table and someone to love us, we are indeed truly blessed, alhamdulillah. So be immensely grateful for the things you do have, strive for those things that you would like and leave the rest in Allah's hands through *du'a*.

Case Study

Sister Uzma is married to Brother Nasir, who gives her permission to do whatever she wants, she has freedom to go where she wants, see the friends of her choosing and she has no shortage of money at her disposal. However, Nasir simply will not help around the house, no matter what. It just doesn't seem to be in his DNA. This issue is causing tension and frustrating Uzma.

I asked Uzma whether Nasir was happy to pay for a cleaner and she said, "Yes, he is happy to pay for whatever help I need, but

---

8 Abu Huraira reported that the Messenger of Allah ﷺ said, "Look at those who are inferior to you and do not look at those who are superior to you, for this will keep you from belittling Allah's Favour to you." (Muslim)

9 Abu Suhayb ibn Sinan narrated that the Prophet ﷺ said, "How amazing is the case of the believer; there is good for him in everything, and this characteristic is exclusively for him alone. If he experiences something pleasant, he is thankful, and that is good for him; and if he comes across some diversity, he is patient, and that is good for him." (Muslim)

I want him to pick up after himself!" I asked her, "Is it reasonable to scream and shout at someone who is not being in the least oppressive and is indeed going out of his way to provide a good life for you?" Then I asked her to look at the whole picture and list all of her husband's fine qualities. After that, she admitted that she had focused too much on one small issue and she promised to be more grateful for her husband.

Case Study

Sister Zaynab looks after her husband, cares for the family home, cooks meals, and is a patient and virtuous wife. Her husband, Brother Idris, complains that she isn't outgoing enough for him. I asked Idris whether this was really such a big deal. I told him of the hadith that the most precious thing in the world was a virtuous woman,[10] and therefore he should feel blessed to have her. Instead of letting such a minor aspect bring the relationship down, I asked him to focus on the many things Zaynab does to please him and bring ease to the family home.

Take a little time to think: Is it such a big deal that I think my spouse has this fault, when they do so much for me?

---

10 'Abdullah ibn 'Amr ibn al-'As narrated that the Prophet Muhammad ﷺ said, "The whole world is a place of precious things and the most precious thing of this world is a virtuous woman (wife)." (Muslim)

What to do next:

> Count your blessings, the little and the large, and thank Allah for all of them.

> Look at your spouse and try and focus on their good characteristics and the positive things that they do.

> Adopt a positive attitude. Remember, the glass can always be half full rather than half empty.

Self-Reflection and Honesty

There is a difference between conscious and unconscious living. We can become so engrossed in day to day living, chores and responsibilities that we may believe we are doing all the right things. But in reality we are not mindful or conscious of the impact of our words or behaviour. This is when we have slipped into what I call the robotic stage. And it's not until something happens that really shakes our world, do we snap out of this auto-pilot mode and realise that there is a problem.

When your relationship reaches a difficult phase, instead of blaming your spouse or pointing out their faults, try looking towards your self first. This requires self-reflection and honesty.

So what does it mean to reflect? Self-reflection is looking closely at your self; making a conscious effort to observe your own character, history, thoughts and feelings. From this, insha'Allah, you will gain an insight into your role in bringing the marriage to the state that it is in at present – where certain behaviours are stemming from, how these affect your spousal relationship, how to change these in order to have a positive effect on the marriage. It is not easy to look at yourself critically or to accept that you may have had a hand in some of the difficulties that are arising between you and your spouse. However, marriage, and indeed life itself, is a training ground for self-growth and development. We must go though this process of inward thought in order to become our best selves.

Sometimes it is useful to remove ourselves from external influences so that we can concentrate on the voice within. This could be finding a quiet place in your lunch hour or some (or all) of the last ten days of Ramadan. The aim is to review ourselves and renew our intentions to go forward in the best possible way.

> *"Those who remember Allah, standing, sitting and lying on their sides, and reflect on the creation of the heavens and the earth: Our Lord, You have not created this for nothing. Glory be to You! So safeguard us from the punishment of the Fire."*
> (Qur'an 3:191)

What to do next:

> Don't let yourself get to the robotic stage. Try and remain mindful at all times; conscious of all your actions and reactions.

> Assess the state of your marriage. What are its strengths and where is there room for improvement? Question yourself as to whether things are so bad? Is it really a problem within the marriage that needs fixing or would a change in perspective be more constructive?

> Honestly evaluate the part that you play in the marriage. Do you behave with patience and good grace? If you are angry, why do you display that behaviour? If you are challenging, why do you do it?

> Look at other people's situations to get a perspective on your own. When you realise what other people go through, you will see what true patience is and insha'Allah, you will develop it in yourself.

> If necessary, find some quiet time away from worldly distractions to go through this process of self-reflection.

Summary

There will be rough patches in married life; it can never be all plain sailing. However, if you both implement these strategies, you can usually steer your self through the storm before it gets any worse.

* Reflect honestly and self critically on the state of your marriage and the effect that this is having on you, your spouse and children.

* Focus on the part you have played in bringing the marriage to its current state.

* Concentrate on ways that you can improve your perspective, speech and behaviour to improve the state of your marriage.

* Make the intention that you want to improve your marriage and strengthen it and pray to Allah to help you achieve it.

❧

Chapter 4

Putting Things Right

Competition

Competition is a surprisingly common occurrence in marriage. We are not always aware that we are being competitive with our spouse and it can have quite a destructive effect. See if the following conversation sounds familiar:

> Husband: *"I'm so tired. I've had such a hard day at work."*
> Wife: *"You think you've had a hard day! You should try being at home all day with the children!"*

This is an example of what I mean by competition. Instead of sympathising and supporting each other, this couple is arguing about who has had the harder day! When you work against each other, even in the most subtle of ways you drive an ever increasing wedge between the two of you and weaken the foundation of the marriage.

Sister Hafsah and Brother Ali said that they felt their marriage was in a rut and that they were drifting further apart. I asked them if they spent quality time together. Hafsah said, "Hardly! I asked him to do the washing up three days ago and he refused. So when he asked me if I would like to come for a walk with him, I refused." Brother Ali interjected, "But you hadn't made me a cup of tea when I asked you to a few days before that."

This marriage had descended into using playground tactics and tit-for-tat behaviour, which had spiralled out of control over time. I asked the couple to reflect on how they sounded and they agreed that it was petty behaviour. I then asked them to think about forgiving, forgetting and making excuses for each other and to see how the marriage would improve after that.

Often this type of competitive behaviour doesn't arise out of nowhere. Usually it is a symptom of another underlying problem.

Sister Ghazala and Brother Imran told me that they had had a massive argument over the weekend. Imran told me, "She usually asks me what I would like to have for dinner on a weekend evening, but she didn't on Saturday, and I didn't like it." Ghazala said, "I chose a shirt for you to wear to work on Friday morning and I asked you if you were happy with the choice. You told me to stop fussing and just take it out. So I didn't ask you about dinner on Saturday. My only crime was to consult you to make sure you were happy and you snapped at me, so I didn't consult you again." That was the start of the argument that started in Saturday evening and arrived in my office on Monday afternoon.

I commented, "I presume there was a beginning, middle and an end to this argument and the incidents with the shirt and dinner were probably the middle." To which Imran responded "Yes, you're right. She's always fussing about the smallest things and I feel overwhelmed and I can't deal with her." Ghazala was bewildered and just asked in a small voice, "Where did that come from?"

I asked each of them to explain their side of the whole story to me and it was as if they were talking about two different marriages. When they realised how the other was actually thinking and feeling, they realised that they had no reason to turn against each other. What Imran thought was fussing, was Ghazala's way of showing her respect for her husband and consulting him about household matters. However, Imran didn't want to be involved in all the trivial household matters and wanted Ghazala to deal with them herself.

This was a classic case of lack of communication and understanding. Ghazala realised that her husband was annoyed by certain things and she has kept quiet over them. Imran has made a point of not snapping at Ghazala all the time, by understanding that her intention is pure.

Now many people would argue that Ghazala's decision was not correct. Why should she have to be the one to give in and keep quiet? Let's look at it another way: Ghazala put 'we' before 'I' and made the effort to refrain from something that she knew annoyed her husband. This immediate sacrifice on Ghazala's part got the couple through a difficult patch. Instead of escalating, the tension in the house eased enough to allow the couple to stay together, discuss the challenges in their marriage and to work on a longer term solution for them both.

Marriage is about teamwork and we expect marriages to have mutual goals and aspirations. In order for the team to succeed, it makes sense that husband and wife each use their own strengths and skills to complement each other and achieve those goals. You each have your own strengths, weaknesses and abilities. By combining the two, you achieve goals that neither of you could achieve single-handedly and that is the beauty of marriage.

What to do next:

> If your marriage has descended into playground tactics and tit-for-tat behaviour, take a deep breath and think. Do you really want to live this way, scoring points and trying to outdo your spouse for the rest of your lives, making both of you miserable in the process? Or do you want to work towards a mutually beneficial partnership?

> Be the one to end the cycle of competitive behaviour. Sympathise with your spouse when they tell you that they have had a hard day, overlook small mistakes and don't keep them in your heart. It will take great personal strength to do that, but the reward will insha'Allah be a happier marriage.

> The disease of individualism is fatal to a marriage. Understand that although you both have your own identities and lives, the situations in which you collectively come together is the marriage. It is a partnership, ordained by Allah ﷻ to provide spouses with comfort and support. This cannot happen when one partner is out for themselves at the expense of the other, and is especially important when children are involved.

Control and Relinquishing It

Relationships are not about who is more qualified in making life choices or who always needs to be in control. It is not a power game. Marriages work best when there is mutual understanding and mutual consultation, and this is not possible when one spouse thinks they can handle things better than the other.

I frequently hear brothers complain, "She treats me like a child. She wants to control me and to her a peaceful life means a life that is run her way only."

Sisters, do you find yourself nagging your husband regularly? Do you feel that if you are not in charge everything will fall apart? Do you feel as if your husband never listens and as a result, those 'told you so' moments are becoming more and more frequent? Do you feel constantly exhausted because you are having to do everything (probably because you think no-one else can do the job as well as you can!)?

This is a situation in which the husband has become too submissive or lax in his responsibilities and the wife has become too assertive. Whether through their own choice or through circumstances, women who are running the ship find themselves exhausted and often become ill trying to carry out the dual role of a husband and wife: running the household, raising a family, providing financially and making all the important decisions.

My advice to sisters is, let go of the need to control and you will achieve more. Your way is not necessarily the right way or the only way, and even if it is, sometimes it is better to allow your husband to learn that for himself rather than impose your will on him. Controlling is a very time- and energy- consuming business and will leave you feeling stressed and anxious. When you understand that you cannot and should not control everything, then you will let go and feel calmer, and also allow for the possibility that you can learn from others.

Case Study

Brother Ayyub left work early to come home and look after the children so his wife, Sister Javaria, could have a well-deserved evening out. After a lovely evening, Javaria got home at 9 o'clock to find the children still awake and the house a mess. Although Ayyub and the children had a great time, Javaria decided to focus on the negative and started telling her husband off for the house being in a mess, the unwashed dishes and the children wearing mismatched pyjamas!

I asked Javaria to focus on the positives. The children had clearly enjoyed themselves, as had her husband. Ayyub spent quality time with the children and she herself had a break. She has a husband who took the time and effort to give her a break and all she could see was a messy house! I explained that complaining and nagging may have resulted in Ayyub washing the dishes that evening but he would be less likely to take time off work for her in the future.

My advice to brothers is: learn what your responsibilities are as a husband, father and son and to carry them out to the best of your ability. Do not leave your wife to carry out her role as well as your own.

Case Study

Sister Ruqayyah told me that she was always managing her husband's life. He just never seemed to achieve anything without being reminded or coaxed into doing it, and on top of all her own responsibilities it was all getting too much for her. She and her husband were heavily involved in helping to organise charity events and although her husband was always happy to get involved, she had to remind him of what he was supposed to be doing every step of the way.

My advice to her was simply: next time, don't remind him. Let him take the responsibility himself and he will either sink or swim. Although she found it difficult not to step in, she took my advice and her husband did not fulfil the role expected of him at the next event. It took some words of reminder from an elder, and the knowledge that he had let people down, for him to finally understand that his responsibilities were his to carry out, and not his wife's.

This one experience changed him more than her words could. This is what I mean by relinquishing control.

What to do next:

> Understand that marriage is not about power and who is right. It is a partnership and this cannot exist where one partner yields control in any way over the other.

> Consider that your way might not be the only way or the right way. Perhaps your standards are unreasonably high. Ask yourself: what is the worst thing that would happen if I let this matter go?

> Ask yourself: how serious would it be if I didn't prompt and remind my spouse about every little thing? As long as the consequences are not dire, then allow him/her to learn from their own mistakes and to take responsibility for their own actions.

> If you do need to speak to your spouse about an issue, do so lovingly and with respect.

> Ask yourself if you are fulfilling your duties and responsibilities completely? Or are you relying on your spouse to help you out or fill in the gaps when you get lazy?

> Think about peace and harmony in the home being more important than control.

Obedience vs. Oppression

When control is taken to an extreme degree then the result is oppression and this is not acceptable in any marriage. However, many couples are confused about the distinction between obedience and oppression and these are, what I like to call, the two 'O's of confusion.

I explain to these couples that the family is like a ship's crew, sometimes there are calm waters and everything is plain sailing, there may be some waves along the way, but these are easily overcome. However, when bad weather hits, it takes the whole crew to weather the storm, or at least two pairs of steady hands, working together, to overcome it. One person cannot do it alone.

Case Study

Sister Aliya recently told me that, despite money being tight in their household, her husband had taken the unilateral decision to begin working a four-day week instead of five days. This put the family into a situation of extreme financial hardship and they were now in a position where they were unable to pay the rent.

Her husband's relationship with the children is also suffering. They no longer respect him as the provider of the household and resent him putting the family in such an insecure position.

Aliya has tried to reason with her husband and he feels that he is the head of the household and the final decision lies with him. He is of the opinion that his wife should be obedient and should not have any input in household decisions.

In cases such as this one, where is the line drawn between obedience and oppression, and just as importantly, who draws that line? Sadly, these are not unusual situations; with many men (and women in some cases) selfishly imposing a 'my way or the highway' attitude on the whole family regardless of the consequences.

Some people have a twisted understanding of the *deen*, while others are simply selfish. In any case, it is contrary to the purpose of marriage for one person to demand obedience from the other or to impose their will on the other. Decisions about jobs, lifestyle and finances affect the whole family and should be taken in consultation with the whole family. In Surah Ash-Shura, Allah ﷻ describes nine of the characteristics of the people who believe and put their trust in Allah (Qur'an 42:37-39). The seventh characteristic is:

'Those who respond to their Lord and establish the prayer,
and manage their affairs by mutual consultation'
(Qur'an 42:38)

The explanation of this ayah[11] includes consultation between husband and wife in domestic matters. The Prophet ﷺ consulted with his Companions and his wives, may Allah be pleased with them all, even though his actions were guided by Allah and he had no need to consult anyone. The act of consulting someone shows that you value their input and opinion, it makes them feel important and creates a sense of partnership, which is exactly what marriage is. A healthy partnership cannot be created when one person issues orders and the other is expected to meekly comply. In fact, this results in loss of love and respect and alters the family dynamics in a way that is irreversible.

True obedience is inclining yourself towards gaining the pleasure of Allah and if that pleasure coincides with the wishes of your spouse, alhamdulillah. If it doesn't, and you are sacrificing yourself and your family to incorrect whims, desires and bad decision making, then that is oppression.

---

11 See footnotes 4578 and 4579 in *The Holy Qur'an: Text, Translation and Commentary* by Abdullah Yusuf Ali.

What to do next:

> Each relationship is unique and it will take some time for each couple to understand how one person's decision affects the whole family.

> Keep the channels of communication open at all times. Consult with your spouse about decisions that you plan to make. If your spouse's decision has affected you adversely and you would have liked to have been consulted about it, then raise this issue with your spouse.

> Refer back to the section on communication about how to approach the matter so that your communication is effective. Explain your concerns at a mutually convenient time, in a calm manner, gently pointing out how the decision has affected you. Be aware of your body language and choose your words wisely. It may be that your spouse never looked at it from your point of view.

Finance and Its Pitfalls

We have discussed earlier about the obligation of a man to provide generously for his family and to spend on them as he spends on himself. We also looked at the desirability of a woman doing without and making sacrifices if her husband is struggling financially and not to make unnecessary demands on his pocket.

Nevertheless, in these times of high cost of living and the emphasis on material wealth, finances are still a cause of much discord in a number of the couples that I see. There are so many things that money cannot buy, such as health, love and contentment and so I always think that it is a shame for something like money to cause a rift between a couple.

The most effective approach to resolving financial issues is to communicate with each other openly and honestly about the situation. Men should be forthcoming about what the household budget is and women should be fair and balanced about communicating what they need it for. This can save a lot of argument and resentment in the long run.

What to do next:

> Set out a budget in writing. Write down the amount that is incoming and then write down a list of essential expenses such as rent, bills, groceries, car insurance and so on.

> Calculate how much is left over to spend each month on non-essentials.

> Discuss what your medium and long term financial goals are: going on holiday, buying a car, setting aside a fund for the children's education, buying a house etc. Set aside an amount towards these goals.

> Stick to your spending limits within the essential and non-essential categories. This may mean reviewing what you think is a necessity, cutting back on eating out or buying new clothes.

> Review the budget every six months.

Intimacy

Intimacy is a very important part of marriage. It is the right of both husband and wife that they find physical enjoyment and fulfilment with each other, without fear or coercion. Intimacy should also not be used as a bargaining tool or a weapon with which to exert control over the other partner; rather it should bring peace and strengthen the love between husband and wife. Each couple is unique in what they find fulfilling, so as long as the bounds of Islam are adhered to, this is a balance that each couple will need to explore for themselves.

Frustrations in this area of your relationship are likely to spill over to other areas of your life and equally, problems in other areas of your life can affect intimacy. Our natural modesty often makes this the most difficult topic to discuss with each other, but my advice would be that it is better to be honest and discuss it openly with your spouse.

The majority of such problems can easily be resolved between husband and wife given time and using effective and loving communication. However, there are situations which are more serious and require professional help. Something that is becoming an increasing problem in society in general, but sadly also among Muslim men, is addiction to pornography.

Pornography, no matter how casually or occasionally viewed, pollutes the heart and mind and destroys relationships. To start with, men spend more and more time on the internet and have less and less interaction with their families. More seriously, they have a warped and unrealistic mind-set regarding women and are consequently unable to be intimate with their wives. If you suspect that there is a problem of this nature in your household, then I would urge you to seek professional help.

What to do next:

> Intimacy is a natural expression that stems from love and security. Nurture the love in your relationship with your spouse and make them feel safe and secure and cherished. Insha'Allah, intimacy will naturally follow.

> In marital relationships, fear Allah ﷻ and stick to the bounds laid down by Him. Refrain from seeing, hearing and speaking indecent things. By preserving your modesty in this way, you will be more fulfilled within your own relationship.

> Remember that you are garments for each other; your job is to honour, protect and beautify your spouse. Respect each others' privacy. Do not disclose the secrets and intimate details of your marriage unless absolutely necessary within the context of mediation.

When In-Laws Become Outlaws

One of the main causes of marital tension, and even breakdown, is the extended family. Marriage isn't just about two people breaking away from their families and forming their own separate unit. It is about bringing together two families in harmony. Unfortunately, this bringing together can sometimes be far from harmonious and a number of negative factors rear their ugly heads at what should be a happy time.

There are a number of changes when two people get married, not only for the couple itself but also for their families. Parents and siblings may feel a sense of loss when their child/brother/sister moves of out of the family home. Now they are not only a son/daughter, brother/sister but also someone else's spouse. This can give rise to feelings of insecurity and jealousy that can manifest themselves as hostility and resentment towards the family member's spouse.

Case Study

Sister Mahnoor came to me, close to tears, with her husband, Brother Arif. Arif and Mahnoor live with Arif's parents and his sister. Mahnoor said that ever since she got married nine months ago, she can't seem to do anything right in her mother-in-law's eyes. She is constantly criticised for the way she dresses, speaks, cooks, cleans, how she spends her spare time, who she goes out with. As if that wasn't enough, whenever there is a disagreement between Arif and Mahnoor, Arif's sister sides with him and Mahnoor feels like she is being ganged up on unjustly. She is desperately unhappy but doesn't know where to turn. She said she expected more support from her husband but isn't getting it.

I asked Arif how he felt. He said he felt 'sandwiched' between his mother and his wife. He said he felt pulled in both directions by emotional blackmail and conflicting loyalties. He thinks that it is impossible to please both his wife and mother and the only way to stay sane would be to leave either his mother or his wife. In the end it just got too much for him to handle and so he just buries his head in the sand and spends more time at work.

This is a very common scenario and there are a number of complex issues here. In order to resolve the situation it is necessary to address the cause of the problems and not the symptoms.

1. The first problem here is that the man's relationship has changed with his mother and sister. He has understandably given more time to his new wife and this has caused his mother and sister to feel insecure and jealous and perceive that they have lost their son/brother to another woman. They are now

acting out through hostility to the new wife.

2. Quite justifiably, the new wife is angry and resentful at being treated this way. She has left her home to be with her husband and expects more support from him. Her anger and resentment boils over as emotional outbursts or blackmail towards her husband or her in-laws.

3. The husband and his father are acting as many men do when family dynamics weaken or begin to crumble. They either act as though everything is fine, ignore the problem or run away from it, for example, by spending more time at work.

As the problem is three-pronged, so the solution also depends on a change of behaviour by all the parties concerned.

Advice for the husband's family:

The bottom line is that we are all Muslims. We must fear Allah and be aware of the sincerity of our intentions as our actions will be judged accordingly. It is one of the basic tenets of Islam that we ought to wish for our fellow brothers what we wish for ourselves.[12] I have dealt with many cases where the daughter-in-law has been disrespected, humiliated and even severely oppressed. The person coming into the family is someone's precious daughter, your son's wife and potentially the mother of your grandchildren. It is a violation of Allah's trust as well as her family's to treat her badly. She should be given due respect and honour. All family members should make the new addition feel welcome and comfortable, especially if they are all sharing the same house.

---

12 Narrated Abu Huraira that the Messenger of Allah ﷺ said, "Do not envy one another, and do not inflate prices for one another, and do not hate one another, and do not turn away from one another, and do not undercut one another in trade, but [rather] be slaves of Allah and brothers [amongst yourselves]. A Muslim is the brother of a Muslim: he does not oppress him, nor does he fail him, nor does he lie to him, nor does he hold him in contempt. *Taqwa* (piety) is right here [and he pointed to his chest three times]. It is evil enough for a man to despise his Muslim brother. The whole of a Muslim is inviolable for another Muslim: his blood, his property, and his honour." (Muslim)

As far as interference is concerned, the married couple are a pair of intelligent and sensible adults. They should be allowed to resolve any issues that arise between them, by themselves. Of course, as elders you may wish to offer the benefit of your experience and wisdom, but this should be done in a loving manner not an admonishing or rebuking one. Extended families should give the couple time and space to adjust to each other and understand that it is natural for the couple to want to spend more time with each other in the early days of the marriage. This should not give rise to jealousy or resentment rather you should be happy that your child has moved on to the next stage in their life and pray for their good in this world and the next.

Advice for the husband:

There are bound to be tensions when the family dynamic changes. It is no good pretending otherwise or hoping that any problems will go away by themselves. Allah ﷻ has made men leaders and problem solvers, so my advice to you is to find a solution by focusing on your roles and responsibilities by accessing Islamic rulings. Islam has defined the rights of a mother and the rights of a wife and how each should be treated.

Your mother has, by the grace of Allah, nurtured you from a state of complete dependence to one of independence. Reassure her that she is still important in your life and that you will always need her. Set aside quality time to spend with your mother and your family. If your family act with injustice towards your wife, then speak to them privately and with kindness. Explain that you are happy with your wife (which is, after all, what every parent wants) and that their treatment of her is not fair and makes you unhappy.

Your wife has the right to be treated well by you and your family. You are her protector and that includes protecting her from hurtful comments and derogatory remarks especially within her own home. If your wife is experiencing hostility from your family, validate her feelings of sadness/anger/resentment and acknowledge that your mother or other family member is not behaving ideally. Reassure her that you are happy with her and tell her what steps you plan to take to remedy the situation. Follow through with whatever you have promised to do.

Advice to daughters-in-law:

Understandably, you are upset at being treated in this way. However, be firm in your intention to please Allah ﷻ, support your husband and keep your personal conduct above reproach. Do your level best to bring peace and unity into the family, not discord. This will mean overlooking and forgiving the faults of others and making excuses for them. As people age or live with chronic illness, they naturally become more temperamental with others. Try not to take it personally. After all, you will age and in time become a mother-in-law yourself. How would you like your daughter-in-law to treat you? Life is not always about what is happening now and what you are going through is a temporary phase which will pass.

You want to please your husband and keep him happy. In doing so you must remember that his family are a part of him. Do not add to his tensions by making him choose between you or his family or emotionally blackmailing him.

And finally, remember that the man you are married to today, with his degree and job and successes is a product of his parents' support and hard work. We only realise this when we become parents ourselves but it takes a huge amount of dedication to bring a child to this stage. So the next time you look at your mother-in-law, don't see the enemy, but a lady who sacrificed her youth to bring up her son – your husband.

Demands and expectations from extended families can also put a great deal of pressure on men as well.

Case Study

Brother Danyal came to me with his wife, Erum. He said that since before the wedding, Erum's family had been making demands on him: to provide an expensive wedding venue, lavish wedding dress, lots of gold jewellery and a high dowry, so that Erum's family would look good in front of their friends.

He continued, "Ever since the day we got married, Erum's mother keeps dropping comments about what other husbands provide for their wives or the fact that I have bought my wife a flat and not a house. Her family is always making me feel that I do not match up to their standards or fit in their social circle. It's like they don't care what kind of person I am, whether I care for their daughter or am kind to her. It's all about being seen to have the right material possessions. If I don't buy what they want, my wife threatens to go back to her father's house. I am being undermined in my role as a provider and decision maker of my household by her family."

Again there are a number of problems here that stem from basically unIslamic behaviour.

1. The wife's family have placed material and worldly considerations over the well-being and happiness of their daughter. They have equated the possession of things with happiness and are making the mistake of comparing what she has with others in their social circle.

2. They are not allowing their son-in-law to be the head of his household by interfering in his lifestyle.

3. The wife is not being supportive enough of her husband.

The solution depends on a change in behaviour from all three parties.

Advice to the wife's family:

When your daughter gets married, she leaves the family home to start a new life with her husband. Although you love your daughter very much, she is now an adult and you must allow her the time and space to adjust to her new role. Constant interference in her life is not helpful in creating peace and harmony in her home. The role of parents is to support and give wise advice, but never to inflame a situation or create more tensions. Sometimes we can be too quick to judge or to take sides especially where our loved ones are concerned. I have heard so many parents telling their daughters to pack their bags and come home at the first sign of trouble without fully understanding the problem or offering any other constructive advice. You have to teach your daughter to be patient, solution focused and not governed by emotions. Marriage is a life long commitment and should be treated as such. As her parents, you can guide her through the rough patches by supporting her in her marriage, listening to her concerns and reminding her of the beauty of compromise in partnership. Leaving the marital home at the first sign of trouble is not the correct path to take unless there is domestic violence or abuse.

Material wealth is no guarantee that your daughter will be happy. Allow the couple to work their way up in life through hard work and perseverance. They will be more appreciative of what they have if they have earned it themselves. Encourage your son-in-law, welcome him and treat him as your own son, but never undermine his position as the head of your daughter's household.

Advice to the wife:

Refer back to your intention for getting married. Are you willing to put in the hard work to create a beautiful lifelong partnership that only gets better with time? Or do you want to behave like a spoilt child.

Creating a family requires hard work, compromises and sacrifice but the result is a deep and fulfilling lifetime of love and security.

Speak with kindness and compassion to your family if they are being unjust to your husband or interfering with the peace of your home life. Support your husband, allow him to feel like the man of your household. Gratefully accept the old banger that he buys you over the luxury car that your father offers to buy you. It speaks volumes about how much you respect your husband and this will increase his love for you. Imagine if your husband went over to his mother's house every day to eat because she cooks better food than you. It would hurt your feelings. You would much rather your husband ate whatever you had made an effort to cook him. Similarly, gratefully accept whatever he is providing you, support him and encourage him. Going back home is only an option if there is abuse and violence and you fear for your well-being, otherwise your home and heart should be with your husband.

In many families, culture and societal norms seem to take precedence over religion. Religion is meant to be easy and allow people to live within what is in harmony with their nature. Some aspects of culture and modern society work to upset that harmony and put immense strain on relationships. For example, in some cultures sons-in-law are treated with more respect than daughters-in-law, which has no place in Islam. Everyone should be treated with respect. In this materialistic age, there is a lot of emphasis on lavish weddings, high dowries and the standard of living of the new couple. The Prophet ﷺ, his wives and his daughters and sons-in-law, may Allah be pleased with them all, all lived in simplicity. They were content with what they had and placed worship of Allah and service to others above all other considerations. There is much we can learn from them.

What to do next:

> Fear Allah in your conduct and behaviour with others, whatever relationship they are to you.

> If you see or hear an injustice being done to your spouse by your family, speak to your family member with kindness and in private and tell them that it makes you unhappy to hear them speak to your spouse in this way.

> If you are aware that your family is making your spouse unhappy, then validate those feelings and acknowledge the situation. Do not ignore it and hope it will resolve itself.

> If a member of your spouse's family speaks to you in a way that you do not like, learn to overlook and forgive small mistakes.

> It is less than ideal for you to be spoken to badly by a member of your spouse's family. However, try not to focus on the here and now and put it into the context of the bigger picture.

Anger

We are all prone to losing our temper sometimes, having a rant and shouting. But we soon cool off, feel bad and make our apologies. However, when losing your temper becomes a regular occurrence or when it escalates into regular outbursts of verbal abuse, hitting objects or people or making other people fearful then it is a serious problem that needs to be urgently addressed.

Sometimes in the heat of the moment, we are so caught up with our own emotions that we fail to recognise what we are doing to the people around us. Anger leaves a negative environment long after the outburst has finished, not only for your spouse but also for the children – an environment of trauma, anxiety and despair.

Anger is corrosive and will eat away at your relationships. It will destroy the love and respect that your family members have for you. Not only does it affect your present relationships, but it is a burden that your children will carry through into their future relationships. If your spouse and children live in constant fear, never knowing when your anger will erupt or how strongly, then they will become anxious and sensitive at best. At worst, they will repeat this abusive behaviour with others.

If you feel that you are always expressing yourself forcefully, through a raised voice and harsh words, then please address these issues. I know that this is easier said than done, but in doing so, you will take a huge step towards creating a strong family bond and giving your children a much better template for their own relationships. The alternative is a broken family, vulnerable and exposed to society, and children with emotional and mental health issues. The choice is yours.

Case Study

Sister Khadijah brought her husband, Brother Qasim, to see me about his anger issues. She told me that he would get angry over trivial matters and he would shout, but that he was never physical. Nevertheless, she was afraid that the next outburst would lead to violence.

After talking to Qasim, I realised that he had witnessed bullying in his home as a child. As a result he was carrying around repressed anger, which was now manifesting itself as anger towards his wife. He would shout at her and she would answer back. He told me that he finds it hard to contain himself when his wife continually answers back, so his anger rises.

I advised Khadijah not to answer back to her husband when she sees his anger heating up, but to leave the room.

I told Qasim to be aware of his escalating emotions. I gave him a range of tools to use for when he feels like he is losing control to rein in his anger and calm him down. These were: reading the du'a for anger (a'udhu billah), counting from one to ten, making wudu or removing himself from the situation. He should then look at the reason why he is angry, whether he is taking it out on the relevant person, whether he is over reacting and to make the connection that his wife has left the room because his behaviour is unacceptable and out of control.

After some counselling sessions and anger management therapy, Qasim and Khadijah were both happier and calmer. Qasim had realised the negative effects of living with someone with anger and was determined not to repeat his childhood patterns in his own married life.

What to do next:

for the angry spouse:

> Think back to your childhood. Are you repeating behaviours and handling situations in the same way that you saw your parents react? Have you witnessed bullying and domestic violence? Are you holding onto repressed anger, which you are now taking out on your family? If any of these things are true then please seek professional help to identify the underlying

causes and work through the symptoms as soon as possible. It is vital to break the negative cycle and give the next generation a positive start in life.

> Think about why you're angry. Did you really mean to take it out on the person you love? Is the object of your anger really somebody, or something else? Rather than lashing out at your spouse, talk to him/her; look to your spouse for support instead.

> If you are constantly angry because of work pressures, for example, then address the underlying cause of your anger. Learn some stress reduction skills, breathing techniques, visualisation and so on, that will lower your general levels of stress.

> Learn to be mindful and aware of your emotions. If you can feel the anger rising in you, your heart beating faster and you are about to open your mouth in a barrage of abuse, then STOP. Work off the anger in any other way: leave the room, get some fresh air, make wudu, recite 'a'udhu billah', go for a run, listen to a relaxing CD.

> Shift your thoughts. If something is making you angry, then stop thinking about it and think about something that makes you happy. For example, if it makes you angry to think about how your husband always leaves his clothes on the floor for you to pick up, then switch to thinking about the time he looked after the children so you could go out. Think about all the good things your spouse has done for you and all their good qualities. Often, a bad patch is exactly that, a temporary situation. There have been lots of good times in the past, and insha'Allah will be in the future.

> Think of your achievements as a team – your home, your children, your shared experiences. This will help to focus on the things that unite you, not on the issues that are dividing you. Also why would you want to jeopardise all your shared achievements for a few moments of anger.

for the spouse at the receiving end:

> If you are subject to abuse and domestic violence then you need to seek professional help immediately. However, if you have a spouse that has occasional anger issues then the following points may help steer the boat through stormy waters while they get help.

> Recognise your spouse's trigger points. If you know what causes them to get angry, then steer clear of doing that.

> Learn to read your spouse's moods. There are often warning signals before an angry outburst, such a moody silence or snapping at little things. Don't choose these times to talk about your problems.

> There is a wonderful reminder from Ibn al-Jawzi in his Sayd al-Khatir:

> "When your companion becomes angry and says something that is unwarranted, you should not take it too hard. His situation is that of a drunken person who is not aware of what is taking place. Instead, be patient, even if it means only for a little while. If you reciprocate his words with harsh words of your own, you become like the sane person who seeks revenge on a madman, or the conscious person who seeks retribution from an unconscious one. Look at him with a merciful eye and pity him for his actions."

for you both:

> Pray and read Qur'an together. What could be more beautiful than standing in front of Allah together? It will soothe, calm and bring you closer to Allah and each other insha'Allah.
> List the positive characteristics about each other instead of focusing on the negatives.
> Both spouses need to give each other space so that the situation can be defused. If neither partner is willing to back down, then the result will be an escalation of continuous arguments without end. Nothing is resolved when both spouses are angry and frustrated.

Symptoms of Conflict

There are several signs that there is conflict between husband and wife, not just the most obvious one which is frequent arguments.

Lack of Compromise

Compromise without resentment is a natural behaviour in a relationship in which there is love, affection and security. Each individual will go out of their way to accommodate and want to please the other as an expression of their love. A relationship in which there is no willing compromise or flexibility is one which is unhealthy and cannot flourish.

For example, brothers can sometimes be very rigid in handling their wives, prohibiting them from seeing their family and friends, going out or working. This in turn leads to the wife feeling angry, depressed and resentful. Equally, some sisters can be uncompromising in their demands as well, which leaves their husband feeling undermined.

Playground Tactics

We all make mistakes and in a loving relationship, each will forgive and overlook the other's little mistakes and shortcomings because in the grand scheme of the marriage they are not worth fighting over.

However, a tit-for-tat attitude and playground tactics are a sign of built-up resentment and bitterness. He says she can't go out with her friends one evening. So she refuses to go to her in-laws house that weekend. This is a vengeful and hurtful cycle that will continue and escalate. It is a childish approach to what should be an adult relationship and it will never have a happy ending.

Forgetting what you are actually arguing about

Another sign of built-up resentment is a constant cycle of arguments that go on for so long, that you can't even remember what made you angry in the first place.

You find yourself shouting at her for forgetting to pick up your dry cleaning and you find yourself shouting at him for leaving his wet towel on the floor. The argument is not about the dry cleaning or the towels but about something deeper.

Ultimatums

How many times have you heard "Get out of my house!" Or "That's it, we're over, I want a divorce!" These words, when said rarely are hard-hitting and hurtful, but when it's the tenth time you've said them this week, they cease to carry weight and become not so much ultimatums, but empty threats.

And finally....

The silent treatment

Sometimes, a bit of peace and quiet is not a bad thing. However, when the quiet goes on for days, or even weeks and the tension in the atmosphere is apparent, it is not alright. When it goes on for three or even six months, that has stopped being conflict and is now oppression, i.e. one partner punishing the other by treating them almost inhumanly.

It is important to recognise, not only that these symptoms are occurring in your household, but also that they are part of a vicious cycle that will only escalate and end in tears... until both of you are willing to break the cycle.

What to do next:

> Remember Allah and recite 'a'udhu billah' when you feel that you are losing control over your tongue and your emotions.

> Never let your ego take over your sensibility. Sometimes, just saying sorry for the sake of Allah to keep the peace may bring a lot of ease, dissolves the conflict instantly and may also cause the other person to reflect on their humility.

> Leave the playground behind and start acting like adults. You will never resolve issues when you are behaving like children. Hitting back at someone who's hurt you leads to more hurt, not resolution.

> Make excuses for each other. Ask yourself whether your partner has just had a bad day and sadly, but as is often the case, it is easier to vent their anger at you than at the boss! Take a deep breath, stay calm and don't take the outburst personally.

> Take some time out. Sometimes, you just need a good rest, some peace and space before you can talk. Issues then become clearer and you are not so reactive or emotional.

> Adopt a positive attitude. Think to yourself, "I want to resolve this. How can I make that happen?"
> Do not trap your partner into a 'captive audience' situation. Attacking your spouse while he or she is driving and there is no place to run, is not a good strategy. It will only lead to more resentment.

Conflict Resolution

Ignoring problems does not make them go away or make them less serious than they actually are. When you brush issues under the carpet and do not deal with them, you get bumps under the rug that just grow with time and one day, you trip over them. My point is that, if and when things happen, you have to deal with them in a manner that makes the situation better not worse.

So what is the best way to deal with conflict? Obviously the key to conflict resolution is communication. Communication and confrontation do not have to be negative or aggressive. In fact, neither of these result in positive resolution to issues. I have outlined below the steps to a successful communication process for conflict resolution.

What to do next:

> If there are simmering issues, deal with them rather than keeping quiet. This is healthier for the relationship in the long run. Don't let things build up and get out of proportion.

> Pick a time that you are both attentive, calm and have the time to talk. Never try to work on issues when you are angry or emotional.

> Stick to the main points. By that I mean the serious issues and the things that have really upset you. "You always forget to take the bins out!!" is not a serious issue so don't bring it up.

> There is no need to bring up every single issue that has ever bothered you. Overlook and forgive the small mistakes, for the sake of Allah and for the sake of your marriage. Life is so much more pleasant without bickering over the petty stuff.

> During the discussion, it is vital that you both speak to each other in a soft tone of voice, using decent speech and relaxed body language.

> Do not resort to name calling or character assassination of each other or extended families, bad speech, swearing or slander. "Evil words are for evil men, and evil men are for evil words; good words are for good men and good men are for good words" (at-Tabari). This does not mean that you cannot say what you need to say, it just refers to the manner in which you communicate your concerns.

> Express your emotions in the here and now, for example "At this moment, I am really angry with you" or "I need some space right now."

> 'I feel' and 'I need' are powerful words in gaining empathy. For example, saying "When you spend so much time working, I feel lonely" or "I need more of your time" is far better than broad accusations such as "You're never here!"

> If your feelings and thoughts are being dismissed or you feel that your partner is not able to really understand what you are saying then try a different form of communication. Things that have worked for my clients include emails, letters and notes. Some people are just better at responding to written communication rather than face-to-face. You have to find what works best for you.

> Listen to your partner. I mean really listen to what they are saying rather than stop talking and start thinking your own thoughts and how you are going to answer them back. There are going to be times when one of you will have to talk about something that is really painful, something that has deeply affected you, or a part of your life where you have been deeply hurt and both spouses have to be open to hearing this.

> The aim of an argument is to resolve it, seek clarity and to draw closer to each other. Keep this in mind when conflicts occur. It is not a game in which one of you has to be the winner. With that attitude, it is likely that you will both end up as losers.

> If no solution is forthcoming and the argument begins to escalate have a contingency plan, for example, leave the room, calmly stating, "This is not working. We are both getting angry. Let's leave it for now and we will discuss it when we are both calmer."

> If arguments are becoming physically aggressive, seek help immediately.

Projection: Building a future

Marriage is a lifelong endeavour and requires constant input from each partner in order to flourish. Of course, there will be rough patches. Nothing of importance is ever gained easily or without tests. The important thing to remember when you are going through a rough patch is that life is not about the here and now and whatever is happening today is not going to last. I have seen many marriages make shaky starts only to blossom into mature and loving partnerships through the hard work and dedication of the couple. I have seen couples sail through the roughest storms because they have held on and wanted to make their marriages work. What these couples had in common was that they focused on the long term and never gave up, no matter how many hurdles they had to cross. They never truly believed that divorce was the better option or that the grass was greener on the other side.

One recent phenomenon I have observed and have already discussed is what I call the 'three month rule'. This seems to be the critical point at which either, or both spouses in a new marriage, think they've given it enough of a chance and feel if it's not working, they shouldn't waste any more time on it.

Three months is not nearly long enough to get to know your partner, their habits (good and bad), their ambitions, dreams, how they want to live or even how to communicate effectively with each other. You might have talked things through before marriage, you may even have met enough times to think you knew your future spouse well, but living with each other opens up a whole new set of challenges and you need time to work through these.

There may be couples reading this right now who are thinking of separating, but I would urge you to focus on, and project into the future. Make the sincere intention of working on your marriage and making it a success. Find common ground; a base on which you can work together to steady the foundations of the partnership.

Case Study

A couple came to me because they were on the brink of divorce, despite the fact that they loved each other. They could not find any common ground on which to begin their marriage and were struggling to find a way forward. Divorce seemed the only option to them. I asked the husband, "If you were to go through with the divorce and remarry, would you still have the same issues?" His honest reply was, "Yes, and probably worse because I love my wife."

By looking to the future and imagining his life with someone else, he realised that he wanted to stay in the marriage and work on it. As a couple, they focused on their future together and overcame the present problems in their marriage.

Sadly, I see many couples who did not think about all the consequences of breaking a marriage and thought that the grass would be greener on the other side. It is easy when you are struggling in your marriage to imagine that being single brings with it a quiet life, emotional, financial and social independence, but further down the line, most people I know would give all of that up to have children and a family life. Many of them have deep regrets about their marriage break ups. Some carry the same issues into their next marriage, others find it harder than they realised to re-marry.

A lot of future heartache can be avoided by thinking level headedly about what you have, how you can work on it and what you would lose by giving it up.

What to do next:

> If you are newlyweds, give the marriage more time. It takes a good while to get to know somebody and to adjust to your new roles. Of course, the first year or so may be difficult, but look back to your intentions for getting married and think about the future.

> Do not base your decisions on what is happening in the middle of a bad patch. Try to understand why this phase has occurred, work your way through it with patience and determination. Remember with the power of du'a, things may change for the better insha'Allah.

> Don't make rash decisions or decisions in the heat of the moment. Calm down and think rationally before you act or make decisions. Remember your teenage years? I am sure we all had impulsive ideas. Think how disastrous it would have been if you acted on them all. Similarly, don't behave like a teenager in your marriage: impulsively and without thought for the consequences to you and other people.

> If you do decide to separate, remember that it is not just the two of you whose lives will be affected. If you have children then this is especially important to consider.

> Finally, look at your marriage as a garden that you tend in order to make it beautiful. You have to work harder in some seasons than in others. Factors outside your control may make your work harder. But you never give up and walk away because it is your garden. Once you have got it to the state you are content with, you can take great satisfaction in your hard work and enjoy it, ready for the next bout of hard work.

Summary

Almost every married couple will face serious issues that shake their marriage. It is in the natural order of life that we will be tested by things that are dear to us. These are the times when you feel helpless and frustrated and your inner turmoil is often taken out on the people closest to you. You don't know where to turn. Any efforts that you do make seem to backfire and the two of you are stuck in a loop of blame, anger and resentment. It seems that it takes too much energy to make an effort to get out of this low point and the only option seems to be to get out of the marriage.

It is precisely at these times, when you cannot seem to move forward, that you both need to stop and reflect. Think beyond the hard times that you are going through. Look back to why you got married and look at what you want to get out of life. Will you be able to achieve peace and satisfaction in your life by destroying a large part of it? If you rebuild a marriage with someone else, can you say that it would be successful?

When you hit a rough patch, this is the time to roll your sleeves up, take a deep breath, ask for Allah's help and do what it takes to repair the marriage. Communicate calmly, give each other space, ask for help from a third party, whatever it takes. But do not give up at the first major hurdle.

Conclusion

❧

Marriage, at its best, is a source of peace, strength and security to the couple. It is from this foundation of love and mercy that children are brought into this world. The family unit provides a cushion to each other from the harshness of the outside world. It covers each others' faults, it protects, it cherishes and loves, gives confidence and self-esteem.

Unfortunately, this ideal doesn't come ready-made. It has to be achieved through hard work by both partners in a marriage, starting from before the couple even get married.

The best results always come from planning and forethought, and marriage is no exception to this rule. To all single people out there looking to get married, I would suggest that you start planning – not just the actual wedding, but the lifetime ahead of it. Distil your thoughts into writing, discuss your feelings with elders and think carefully and rationally about what you are embarking on and who with.

Once you are married, the actual hard work begins. No matter how much you have spoken to a person before marriage, living with someone is a whole different ball game. It will take time to adjust to your new roles and responsibilities, and allowing the idea that you should no longer act and behave in your own best interests, but in the team's best interests to sink in. Basic courtesy, decency and good character go a long way in keeping marriages healthy.

All marriages will hit stagnant patches where you don't feel as close to your spouse. These can be worked through by communication and self-reflection. Keep your lines of gentle and effective communication open so that you do not give resentment an opportunity to build up. There is a lot of wisdom in looking to your own self in times of trouble by exercising patience and gratitude and looking at your own faults before pointing the finger at someone else's. As husband and wife, you are a team. That means you are on the same side and should be working together not against each other.

Of course, there will be times that more serious issues creep into the marriage, some of which are beyond your control. This is the time to stop and assess the marriage and your behaviours. Fear Allah in your conduct towards your loved ones and follow Allah's guidelines with respect to your relative roles and responsibilities. Many marriages fall by the wayside because of a lack of proper understanding of how men and women should behave within a marriage according to the *deen*.

There is great reward in submitting to the roles that Allah in his wisdom has ordained for us. For wives, it is important to understand that when you have children, you are their primary teacher. The future of the *ummah* is in your hands and this is a privilege as well as a responsibility. Your path in marriage is not to be hostile or competitive but to provide a loving and secure home for your partner and your children. Embrace this role for the sake of Allah ﷻ and the rewards will be immense.

Husbands, treat your wives kindly. This cannot be stressed enough. Muslim women, especially these days, face great pressures from the outside world. Your role is to provide generously, to protect, to support and to cherish her. Always take your wife's feelings into consideration and consult her about decisions that affect the whole family. Take direction from the example of the Prophet ﷺ as a husband. Kindness, mutual understanding and flexibility will always yield better results than harshness, rigidity and lack of consultation.

Do not be shy about seeking help for your marriage. Often the issues that someone experiences may actually stem from childhood issues and this needs to be handled professionally.

Our greatest, most fulfilling relationship is the one with our Lord. We may try to find solace in people and things yet this is as substantial as a mirage in a desert. Having true reliance on Allah ﷻ is the anchor of our success.

I pray that the advice that I have provided in this book has been of help to those seeking to get married, to those starting out in their married lives and to those struggling with their marriages. As human beings, we will always make mistakes and fall into error, but we must learn to trust in Allah and lift ourselves up again because that is the nature of this life.

The strong person is the one who desires to learn from their mistakes and tries to resolve the issues at hand with humility. The end goal is to please Allah ﷻ and, through achieving this, to attain Jannah.

About the Author

Afshan Khan (Umm Asim) is an Islamic counsellor, NLP life coach, youth mentor and parenting advisor with thirty years of experience. Her main work centres around marital issues, family disputes, teenage problems, domestic violence and mediation.

She is saddened by the alarming rise in divorce levels over the past few years within the Muslim community and is pro-active in taking steps to remedy this. She passionately believes that strong marriages and good parenting are the foundations of a successful society that is confident in its identity, productive in this world and prosperous in the next.

To this end, she has set up Sukoon healing, which offers face-to-face and telephone counselling and mediation services for sisters and couples. In addition she runs a host of support groups and workshops for sisters at all stages of their lives including:

- Pre-marriage workshops
- Skills for marriage workshops including effective communication, dealing with extended family, cooking and housekeeping skills
- Parenting workshops
- Support groups for divorced women
- Personal development workshops including confidence building, assertiveness and health support

Umm Asim has helped literally hundreds of people throughout her career and continues to be as busy as ever. You can find out more about her, the work that she does and the heartfelt testimonials of people whose lives she has transformed, by the grace of Allah ﷻ at:

Website: www.sukoon.org.uk
E-mail: afshankhan@sukoon.org.uk
Facebook: Sukoon Healing
Twitter: Ummasim1
Blog [wordpress]: afshankhan1